"This book is a terrific r _____ eir
relationship with God than lackluster routines and complacent rituals. Lisa is
both an engaging guide and an experienced practitioner, using Scriptures and
stories, to lead us through eight characteristics needed to fuel a dynamic and
passionate life with God. With questions for self-reflection, discussion, and
practical application, this book can be used individually or in community with
others to gain fresh insights, develop greater depth, and experience fulfilling joy
in our life with God."
—Carolyn Taketa, host of the Small Group Network podcast *Group Talk*

"Lisa Smith's latest book is a treasure. It will draw you closer to God and will
ignite your heart with passion for Him. Her insight and beautiful storytelling
makes every section of this book delightful to read!"
—Stacy DeWitt, executive director of James Storehouse

"As a much as this book is about character and stories of particular women,
it also a look at a set of eight people who knew and loved their Lord—people
who allowed themselves to be shaped by Him over and above their culture and
their circumstances. It is my hope that Lisa's insights into these 'great eight'
propel you towards habits of godliness—putting you in a place to receive
grace and fall more deeply in love with your savior—and that in His love you
might be re-shaped and re-formed. Our love for Christ and our willingness
to follow Him by letting Him shape, form, and mold our character at the level
of daily habits and practices is a way that every believer made in His image
(women and men) proclaims His love to a world gone mad."
—Robert William Alexander, author of *The Gospel-Centered Life at Work*

"This book is a slim treasure, packed with practical inspiration for the
passionate Christian life. Utilizing the stories of some of the unsung heroines
of Scripture, *Godly Character(s)* will be a trustworthy companion on the quest
of devotion."
—Lanier Ivester, writer and speaker at LanierIvester.com

GODLY CHARACTERS

INSIGHTS FOR SPIRITUAL
PASSION FROM THE LIVES
OF 8 WOMEN IN THE BIBLE

LISA SMITH

GODLY CHARACTERS

INSIGHTS FOR SPIRITUAL PASSION FROM THE LIVES OF 8 WOMEN IN THE BIBLE

SQUARE HALO BOOKS

In Christian art, the square halo identified a living person presumed to be a saint. Square Halo Books is devoted to publishing works that present contextually sensitive biblical studies, and practical instruction consistent with the Doctrines of the Reformation. The goal of Square Halo Books is to provide materials useful for encouraging and equipping the saints.

©2018 Square Halo Books, Inc.
P.O. Box 18954
Baltimore, MD 21206
www.SquareHaloBooks.com

Scripture quotations are from the *Holy Bible: The New International Version* (Grand Rapids, MI: Zondervan, 2011).

ISBN 978-1-941106-11-2
Library of Congress Control Number: 2018964399

Printed in the United States of America

CONTENTS

This book is dedicated
with love to my husband Steve
and my sons Alex and Ryan.
Thank you for always loving
and supporting me.

*I would also like to sincerely thank
my good friends Carolyn Taketa
for her invaluable input in
the early stages of this project
and Ned Bustard for his work
to improve it in the final stages.*

INTRODUCTION

PASSION. We watch it drive our favorite sports teams to remarkable athletic exploits in massive arenas, we cringe as it tears apart the marriage of our best friend, we empathize as it propels Christian saints toward torture and persecution in hostile lands, and we ache when it fades from our most important relationships. Passion can make us endure more than we could imagine, accomplish things we thought impossible, and feel something so strongly it becomes a full-blown obsession. Passion moves humans in ways nothing else can. If we could bottle and sell it, we would have retired to the Cayman Islands by now.

Motivational speaker and author of books on leadership John Maxwell calls passion "fuel for the will."[1] Passion is an ardent affection for and devotion to something or someone. It directs both the emotions and the will toward achieving the object of its desire, and its power lies in the fact that it will not be stopped. True passion is an all-consuming fervor that will make things happen, overcome obstacles, and persevere through challenging times. It will not be waylaid by fatigue, impediments, or trials, and has no part with laziness, distraction, or apathy. It carries on when the road ahead is uncertain, confusing, or menacing, pursuing its object regardless of cost. Passion makes things happen. And we know it when we feel it.

But often our Christian experience feels just the opposite—commonplace, unfruitful, anything but passionate. We become bored with our spirituality, feeling like we are simply going through the motions, missing out on both the personal transformation and the effective ministry that Jesus seems to promise. Or, worse, we struggle even to feel the desire for something more. Years of disappointment, heartache, busyness, or missteps have sapped both our desire for a passionate Christian life and our energy to pursue it. How can we recover our spiritual passion? Perhaps the latest popular Bible study or Christian speaker or weekend conference will jump-start our lagging relationship with God. Perhaps the key we need is just within reach, hidden in the pages of the latest Christian bestseller or buried in the Sunday sermon our pastor delivered last week. Perhaps it cannot be found.

I first became interested in the concept of spiritual passion when I encountered the writings of the Reverend George Whitefield. An eighteenth-century Anglican minister in England, Whitefield could not have been more different from me, but something about his life and ministry grabbed my attention. Originally aspiring to become an actor, Whitefield ended up as a globe-trotting evangelist, setting records throughout his lifetime for attendance at his open-air meetings. Zealous, captivating, and unorthodox in his extemporaneous style of preaching, Whitefield's sermons and prayers sparked revival wherever he went in Great Britain and the American colonies during the eighteenth century, revitalizing what had become for many a lifeless, conventional religion. He changed the face of eighteenth-century Christianity by inspiring his listeners to an authentic, personal relationship with Jesus, despite enduring relentless persecution and slander from those who did not like his enthusiasm. When he died in Newburyport, Massachusetts, on September 30, 1770, his funeral procession stretched more than a mile.[2]

Reading his personal journals, I was struck by how different Whitefield's experience with God was from mine, even though I had been a Christian for years. My spiritual experience was far from the thrilling Christian life I was reading about in Whitefield's diary. In fact, my relationship with God appeared to be resoundingly mediocre. What was Whitfield's secret? As far as I could tell from his journals, Whitefield had an insatiable drive both to draw closer to God and to see the Lord glorified in his ministry to others. Although suffering with sickness and fatigue while conducting a preaching tour of the American colonies in 1740, Whitefield writes in his journal during a private time with God: "My body was weak, and my appetite almost gone; but my Lord gave me meat, which the world knows nothing of. Lord, evermore give me this bread!"[3] I realized that what was missing from my spiritual life was the key ingredient in Whitefield's—*passion.*

But if passion is our goal, then why isn't this book called *Godly Passion?* Simply put, it is because passion is not our goal. Passion is the *fruit* of a godly life in the same way that passion is the *fruit* of a godly marriage, not its goal. We all know that if a marriage lacks passion, the solution is not to drum up passionate feelings. Instead, passion will result from the hard work we put into the relationship.

But how does one develop spiritual passion? When we examine the life of Jesus, we see that His passion flowed out of a life of godly discipline that was both internally and externally focused. The gospel writer Luke notes many instances of Jesus turning inward to spend time alone with His Father in prayer before undertaking outwardly significant events in His ministry. He takes time to seek the Father before His baptism by John (Luke 3:21–22), before choosing His disciples (6:12), before asking the question that would lead to Peter's confession that He was the Christ (9:18), before the Transfiguration (9:28–29), before teaching His disciples what is commonly called The Lord's Prayer (11:1), and before His betrayal and crucifixion in Gethsemane (22:41). Jesus understood that God's power begins by entering our hearts and lives, and then pours out into the world. As followers of Jesus, our lives can become stagnant and self-centered when we focus exclusively on cultivating internal passion. Conversely, when we direct our efforts primarily toward fervent ministry and service, we risk becoming burned-out and frustrated. Real, spiritual passion comes from lives growing in godly character that manifests itself both inwardly and outwardly.

Character is a word that in our day seems more related to sitting up straight and eating your broccoli than to the concept of passion. Yet in these pages, I attempt to show that spiritual passion flows from character. This book higlights eight key character traits—four that help us develop an inward drive toward God and four that accomplish in us an outward release of His love and power. Internally, we will seek to develop *devotion, courage, renewal,* and *vision;* externally, we will pursue *initiative, nonconformity, tenacity,* and *generosity.* Maturity and growth in these godly characteristics will produce a deeper, more sustained intimacy with God as well as an outward looking, powerful faith. Of course, attempting to distill life experiences into words on a page is always fraught with limitations, but we know as Christians that spiritual growth in any area can happen if we join an authentic desire for heart change with new understandings and behaviors. The Holy Spirit can accomplish amazing growth in our lives when we partner with Him in changing our minds and hearts.

And since I teach literature for a living, I couldn't resist using stories to make the concepts in this book more accessible and appealing, as the Bible itself does.[5] Thus, each attribute of passion is discussed in light of a godly character in the Bible who displays that trait. I've deliberately chosen more obscure people in the Bible to help us bring fresh eyes to their stories. These followers of God will clarify for us the primary obstacle to each characteristic, the concrete choices we must make to develop them, and the results we can expect to see as we mature in these characteristics. At the end of the book are discussion questions for a group (or for personal reflection), application ideas, and suggested steps for deeper growth.

In John's account of heaven, God Himself inhabits the Holy City, and from his throne flows an endless river of life. Heaven's river is symbolic of how spiritual passion for God can flow through us and into the world. John describes the scene this way in Revelation 22:1–2:

> Then the angel showed me the river of the water of life, as clear as crystal, flowing from the throne of God and of the Lamb down the middle of the great street of the city. On each side of the river stood the tree of life, bearing twelve crops of fruit, yielding its fruit every month. And the leaves of the tree are for the healing of the nations.

My prayer is that the Holy Spirit will use this book to unlock your passion for God and for pursuing Him with all that you are. May we experience the power of God's heavenly river of the water of life flowing into us and out to the world.

01: DEVOTION

CONQUERING DISCONTENTMENT

THE ROMANCE BEGAN AUSPICIOUSLY. The young woman loved the young man, she desired his embrace and his kisses. She longed to steal away with him so they could be together forever. For his part, he praised her beauty, preferred her to all others, and promised her they would have a life together. Their friends rejoiced in the union, celebrating the love between the two youths. But one night, the young man disappeared. Frantic, the maiden searched the city, asking policemen strolling their beat if they had seen him, scouring the streets for a hint of his whereabouts. Finally, she discovered him, but her delight was short-lived, as he disappeared again, and this time even the maiden's friends counseled her to forget him—certainly she could find someone else just as wonderful. But the young woman would not be dissuaded. Determined, she pursued her lover and ultimately found him in a garden, among the spices, and the reunion affirmed their reciprocal love and affection. He had been waiting for her, not hiding, intent upon a life committed to her and her alone. Their mutual passion was eternal, as strong as death, and could not be quenched; their union would be a perpetual testimony to the power of love.

This familiar tale, while it is the plot of countless romantic movies and books throughout history, is also the storyline of the Old Testament book Song of Songs. While interpretation of the book has varied considerably over the centuries, the devotion these two young lovers show toward each other has consistently moved readers of the tale. The lover proclaims his undying passion for his beloved with pronouncements such as this: "You have stolen my heart, my sister, my bride; you have stolen my heart with one glance of your eyes." Similarly, the maiden testifies to the strength of their commitment: "I belong to my beloved, and his desire is for me."[1] The closing chapter of the book provides a moving declaration of the power of their unswerving fidelity to each other:

> Place me like a seal over your heart,
> like a seal on your arm;
> for love is as strong as death,
> its jealousy unyielding as the grave.[2]

Such affection and mutual devotion has resonated with readers across cultures and centuries, making Song of Songs one of the most quoted biblical books at the most dedicated of all unions, ceremonies of marriage.

Our discussion of growth in the Christian life must begin here, with the attribute of devotion, as true devotion is the foundation for a life of spiritual passion. Devotion is deep dedication to a person or a cause, a sincere attachment. Devotion implies loyalty, steadfastness, and unwavering fidelity. The word has religious connotations because of the intensity of the dedication it connotes; *consecration* is not too strong of a synonym. We expect true devotees to stay the course through thick and thin, to offer themselves and all their resources to the one they follow. Devotion assumes complete allegiance.

But most importantly, the heart must be involved to produce true devotion. Perhaps this aspect of devotion is most easily understood when devotion is compared to the concept of commitment. Commitment does not have to involve the heart—we can be committed to a job, a volunteer organization, a diet, a clothing company, and not feel an emotional connection to the object of our commitment. But devotion assumes an emotional connection that goes beyond grit-our-teeth commitment. Devotion assumes that we care.

Interestingly, for a time, both devotion and commitment will produce a similar outcome—either one can maintain marriages, attain athletic accomplishments, or produce remarkable professional achievements. Yet, eventually, the lack of emotional connection in disinterested commitment will reveal a shaky foundation. Swedish tennis great Bjorn Borg had won six U.S. Open titles and five Wimbledon championships by the time he was twenty-five years old, yet left professional tennis a year after his last Grand Slam win. Years later, when asked about his seemingly premature departure from tennis, Borg remarked, "I still played good tennis but I did not have the same focus that I had for many years. I always gave 100 percent and loved to win and hated to lose but if you lose that little bit of an edge it is very difficult to do well. Something was missing and for me as a person that is not right."[3] What was missing for Borg was devotion to the game, and commitment could not make up for it. Commitment alone cannot sustain one indefinitely; if our personal feelings become divorced from what we are pursuing, we will eventually lose our fervor and drift away from our goal.

Conversely, our emotional bond with the object of our devotion produces a strong foundation for sustained focus and pursuit. It is this heart element that makes devotion so foundational to a life of spiritual passion. The heart will maintain and nourish passion longer than any other motivation, even such effectual ones as desire for success or fear of failure. As the writer of Proverbs cautions, "Above all else, guard your heart, for everything you do flows from it."[4] When our hearts are committed to something, we are devoted in every sense of the word.

Devotion is particularly important for the follower of Jesus because the Christian life is above all else a relationship. God desires to enter a love relationship with humanity that will culminate in perfect union for all eternity. If we desire a religion based on human works, complex philosophies, or matrices of right and wrong behaviors, there are other religions that will be more satisfying. Following Jesus requires a heart commitment, and devotion more than any other attribute brings the heart into our pursuit of God and thus provides the basis for a passionate spiritual life.

OBSTACLE TO DEVOTION: DISCONTENTMENT

In the New Testament book of Luke, we encounter a woman who demonstrates extreme devotion to God in the face of circumstances that easily could have led her down a very different path. Luke recounts for us the story of Anna, a widow who has lived in the temple in Jerusalem for decades, worshiping, fasting, and praying. She appears in only three verses of Scripture, but her story reveals a woman who is an example of true devotion. In the presence of Jesus' parents and other worshipers, Anna meets Jesus when He is only months old and gives thanks to God the Father for Jesus, offering prophetic words concerning His future role in redeeming the people of Israel:

> There was also a prophet [in the temple], Anna, the daughter of Penuel, of the tribe of Asher. She was very old; she had lived with her husband seven years after her marriage, and then was a widow until she was eighty-four. She never left the temple but worshiped night and day, fasting and praying. Coming up to them [Joseph and Mary] at that very moment, she gave thanks to God and spoke about the child to all who were looking forward to the redemption of Jerusalem.[5]

Anna certainly evidences a sincere devotion to God, spending her days continually worshiping and praying in the temple. In fact, in Anna's case, the word *consecrated* is very appropriate. She has chosen to consecrate her entire life—all her resources, desires, hopes, and her future—to worshiping God through praise and intimacy. That is devotion.

Yet, her devotion might surprise modern believers because it seems to come out of nothing. There is very little about Anna's life that we would envy. She has lived as a widow for decades, losing her husband after only seven years of marriage. The passage does not mention children or other relatives, so it is possible that Anna is alone in the world. From what we know of the culture in which she lived, as a widow, Anna occupies a position of little power or influence, as women at the time typically had fewer legal rights than men, especially regarding property ownership and monetary earning power. She undoubtedly struggles with financial need and loneliness. She is a woman forgotten and insignificant, living out her life on the fringes of society.

Even worse, Anna occupies a marginalized position in the temple in which she chooses to spend her life. This might surprise us, impressed as we may be by her decision to devote her life to the worship of God. Surely her commitment is beyond question and a testimony to all. Yet, every day of her life, as she worships and prays, Anna has to watch as numerous people file past her into a more holy temple court than the one she inhabits. It is called the Court of Israel, and Anna is not allowed inside. Why isn't Anna allowed into this more sacred court? Certainly her dedication to the worship of God should ensure her inclusion. Simply put, Anna is excluded from the Court of Israel because she is a woman. As a female Hebrew, Anna is confined to the Court of the Gentiles, which was the outermost court of the temple, and the Court of Women. The Court of Israel is closed to her because of her gender, and the Court of the Levites, the most holy place, is open only to Levitical priests.[6]

For the casual temple attendee, perhaps this limitation was unimportant. But for Anna, who has devoted her life to ministering to God, this restriction quite likely rankles. What must she feel, a woman who has given up everything for the worship of God, when she sees others entering the more holy place of God's manifest presence while she is kept outside? Powerless in society, alone in the world, and barred from drawing physically nearer to God—these are Anna's circumstances. Have you ever been in a similar place? Most of us can empathize with Anna because we have experienced times when we have felt powerless, alone, or hindered from what we truly need. These experiences can send us spiraling toward the main obstacle to devotion—discontentment. Discontentment is a sense of being dissatisfied or unfulfilled. We may feel we are missing out on things or begin to see our life as less than what it should be, or as less than what we deserve. We can begin to spend our time criticizing and complaining, or envying those who seem to have what we want.

Why doesn't my boss appreciate my efforts at work? Why do I have to struggle with financial debt while so many others are born with silver spoons in their mouths? Why is my spouse so selfish and uncompromising? Why is poor health always dogging me? Why is my church so backward and unsupportive? Questions like these churn through our minds as we spend our resources dealing with the various issues we face and the seeming restrictions they place on us. And, perhaps even worse, we can end up wasting even more time dealing with the bitterness and emotional turmoil these limitations often produce in us. We can even grow discontented with God Himself if things do not eventually go our way or we feel He has denied us something we need or deserve.

I will admit that I have struggled with discontentment over issues both big and small: lack of appreciation at work, financial limitations, never-ending physical therapy visits to fix weekend-warrior injuries, even dissatisfaction with how well my children are performing on their most recent sports teams. Still, I am always somewhat surprised when discontentment gets ahold of me because it seems only logical that our modern American culture of immediate gratification should protect us from the trap of discontentment. Money can be borrowed, promises can be broken, and people can be disregarded in our pursuit of what we want. Yet, somehow, we all still suffer from the universal human experience of frustrated desires. As the New Testament writer James has reminded readers throughout the centuries, "What causes fights and quarrels among you? Don't they come from your desires that battle within you? You desire but do not have, so you kill. You covet but you cannot get what you want, so you quarrel and fight."[7] We all struggle with encountering situations in which we cannot fulfill our desires.

Discontentment is an obstacle to true devotion in two ways. First, discontentment is essentially a way of saying that God is not providing for us or loving us as He should. Since we know from passages such as Romans 8:28 that God's love for us is perfect and that He will work out all things for our good, giving in to discontentment denies the truth of God's love and care for us. This is not to say that we should not have a holy discontent with the sin and evil that exist in the world and that often impinge quite painfully on our lives. Certainly, we should strive against the works of the devil, who Jesus notes in John 10:10 came to steal, kill, and destroy. We should not ignore or explain away the pain and suffering that often come from difficult situations. Unhealthy discontentment, however, shifts the focus from combating the evil of the world to questioning God's love for us and thus easily derails our devotion to Him, particularly because it damages our emotional connection with our divine Lover. It is hard to feel love for someone who you believe is hurting or ignoring you.

Discontentment also harms our devotion to God by placing us at risk of missing key parts of God's plan for our lives. It is difficult to sense and follow God's leading when we are continually complaining about and trying to change what He is doing. In his book *Life Without Limbs*, author Nick Vujicic recounts his experience of living without arms or legs. As one can imagine, Vujicic struggled intensely at times with even the most routine tasks, and if anyone could be forgiven for succumbing to discontentment, it would be Vujicic. In his book, Vujicic recalls how his unhappiness led him to "hit a wall" as he struggled to deal with the reality of his disability, even once attempting to drown himself.[8] However, Vujicic went on to become an international motivational speaker, best-selling author, mentor, husband, and father. Vujicic explains that he came to realize that "beyond my own struggles there was a purpose for my life awaiting me. And it has proven to be far, far, *far* beyond anything I ever could have imagined."[9] As Christians, we have God's promise in Ephesians 3:20 that He can do "immeasurably more than all we ask or imagine." God's plans for us are always far beyond even our wildest dreams, and our best moments in life are when we embrace what our Father has for us. Unfortunately, when we live in discontentment, God's amazing purposes and promises are lost to us because our focus is instead on what we believe we are missing. We overlook opportunities to move forward into the new things God has for us, and these missed chances for growth and encounter weaken our devotion to Him.

TOOLS OF DEVOTION

Nick Vujicic's life would have been very different had he not found a way to overcome discontentment. Like Vujicic, Anna also is able to resist discontentment and develop a passionate devotion to God. What might be her secret? I believe we can identify four key elements in Anna's life that help nurture and sustain her devotion to the Lord.

1: LIVING IN GOD'S PRESENCE

The first key to developing devotion can be found in Anna's unceasing physical presence in the temple. Anna *lives* in the presence of God—twenty-four hours a day, seven days a week. What do we know about the presence of God? It is the place from which blessing and healing flow. As Psalm 16:11b reminds us: "In Your presence is fullness of joy; At Your right hand are pleasures forevermore."[10] God's presence reinvigorates us, rejuvenates us, and reorients us. In His presence we become aware through the Holy Spirit of our wrong ideas, impure motives, and hurting places. God's healing, empowering presence brings transformation and motivation to our lives. Anna makes a conscious decision to abide in God's presence continuously, and thus she is continuously in the place to receive God's blessing and favor.

Sadly, the very real power and blessing of being in God's presence, both corporately and individually, is often underestimated by modern believers. We don't think it really matters if we skip church or miss our personal time with the Lord. However, when we miss those opportunities to experience God, we miss the blessings of healing and wholeness that come from spending time with the Lover of our souls—blessings that cannot be received from any other source.

A beautiful biblical image of this dwelling in God's presence comes to us in the Song of Songs. As noted above, the young lover and his beloved meet in a garden and mutually declare their eternal love. The lover identifies his bride as "a garden locked up, my sister, my bride; you are a spring enclosed, a sealed fountain." The bride is enclosed and secured because she is open to only one person—her lover. Later in the chapter, she invites her lover to join her with the words, "Awake, north wind, and come, south wind! Blow on my garden, that its fragrance may spread everywhere. Let my beloved come into his garden and taste its choice fruits."[11] The bride is anticipating a beautiful time of intimacy with her lover. As this biblical picture reveals, devotion is strengthened by spending significant time in the presence of our eternal Lover.

While we may not live continually in the church as Anna did, we can still work into our lives a commitment to spending time in God's presence. Rising early, turning off the television or laptop at night, or declining a lunch offer can all provide precious moments to be alone in God's presence and attend to Him. Finding a small group that will include the whole family or attending a church that offers multiple worship times are ways to work into our lives a corporate experience of God's presence. As we spend time in His presence, His love and blessing will flow toward us, and our love and devotion will increase as a result.

2: WORSHIP

A close friend of mine lost her mother unexpectedly. Enjoying family time at the beach one day, her mother passed into glory the next. To make matters even more difficult, my friend and her husband, pastors of a newly formed church, had agreed months earlier to host a multichurch worship service on the evening of the day that was scheduled for her mother's funeral. Of course my friend would be in no position to host the service after such an emotional event and would have to cancel, right? Wrong. When I asked her how she found the strength to fulfill her commitment to the worship service, she answered, "I can think of no better place to bring my pain and begin my healing than a place in which Christians are gathered together to worship and exalt the Lord."

What my friend recognized was the supernatural nature of worship. Worship is exalting and blessing God for who He is—good, wise, loving, kind. It is acknowledging with single-minded focus the supreme beauty, majesty, and power that is our God. It is singing and speaking the worthiness of God, or acknowledging His absolute preeminence with mute adoration. It is offering all that we are for the glory, honor, and blessing of the Lord, trumpeting His splendor and magnificence throughout creation. Anna worships in the temple "day and night," and the presence of worship in her life deepens her devotion.

Worship is a discipline that engenders devotion in our hearts for several reasons. First, worship is the most selfless act we can commit as fallen creatures because at its base, worship requires us to focus outside ourselves. It is impossible to acknowledge the worth of someone else and at the same time compliment yourself. As the New Testament writer James asks his readers, "Can both fresh water and salt water flow from the same spring?"[12] Certainly not. When we focus on the Lord in worship and praise, we step outside ourselves and move into the selflessness that God desires from us.

Second, worship increases our devotion by giving us a larger, more accurate picture of God and reality. Worship gives us God's perspective. As we acknowledge and rejoice in His attributes and the truths contained in the Bible, our perspective shifts from our own limited understanding of the world and reality to God's bigger version of reality. When we worry that God does not see our pain, we praise Him for His promise in Psalm 10:17: "You, Lord, hear the desire of the afflicted; you encourage them, and you listen to their cry." When we wonder if God has power to help us, we remember Jeremiah 32:17: "Ah, Sovereign Lord, you have made the heavens and the earth by your great power and outstretched arm. Nothing is too hard for you." When we doubt God's willingness to forgive our failures, we claim the promise in John 1:9 that He is "faithful and just" to forgive our sins. Worshiping God according to the truths of His Scripture reorients our perspective, bringing it in line with God's ultimate reality. And having God's perspective opens us up to receiving God's revelation. As Psalm 50:23 notes, "He who sacrifices thank offerings honors me, and he prepares the way so that I may show him the salvation of God."[13] When we share God's perspective, we see reality through His eyes and are open to receiving insight from Him, moving us to greater devotion.

Worship also channels God's power in our lives, drawing us to the One who has authority over all creation. Perhaps no greater example of this exists in Scripture than Joshua and the Israelites' siege at the walls of Jericho. In Joshua 5:13–6:5, God commands the Israelites to march around the city of Jericho in a procession of praise instead of besieging the city in battle garb. God's power is then revealed when He causes the city walls to fall. Anne Graham Lotz, noted speaker and author and daughter of the famous evangelist Billy Graham, asserts the power of worship in her book *My Heart's Cry*: "Whenever I have control of a meeting where I will be speaking, I arrange to have hymns and choruses of praise precede the message as a means of cleansing the invisible, spiritual atmosphere, giving Him absolute authority over the proceedings. In some supernatural way, praise ushers the authority of God into any given situation."[14] God's power and authority follow our praise and draw our hearts to Him.

Lastly, worship strengthens our devotion because it cements our understanding of our identity in Christ. The apostle Peter recognized this truth: "But you are a chosen people, a royal priesthood, a holy nation, God's special possession, that you may declare the praises of him who called you out of darkness into his wonderful light."[15] Worship is in our nature as born-again lovers of God. We were saved to bring glory to the One who saved us, both individually and corporately. As songwriter Twila Paris and worship scholar Robert Webber note in their book on worship, "Worship reveals the very nature of the church, for the church at worship is a prefigured experience of the ultimate goal of human history."[16]

Evangelism, Bible study, discipleship, service—these valuable Christian practices will have no place in heaven. Only worship will remain as we spend eternity pouring out our love and devotion to our glorious and majestic King of Kings. Thus, the worship we experience now in space and time validates who we are as God's people—His beloved, cherished bride, redeemed to give Him honor and praise.

Anna worships in the temple, and we, too, can worship God corporately with others or by ourselves individually. Perhaps we can use the first ten minutes of our personal devotional time to sing our favorite worship song or read through a Psalm of praise. Maybe we can interrupt our drive to or from work to drop by our church prayer room and spend time praising God for who He is. Twenty minutes can be set aside on a Sunday to lead a family worship time by singing along with a worship DVD. Working worship into our lives increases our devotion and passion for God as it broadens our perspective and shifts our focus to the One who redeems and blesses us.

3: PRAYER

Along with worship, prayer is a discipline that Anna is known for practicing. Certainly the topic of prayer warrants its own chapter, if not its own book. My favorite quotation on prayer comes from the early church father Augustine: "True, whole prayer is nothing but love."[17] Contemporary writer Richard Foster elaborates: "My first counsel is simply a reminder that prayer is nothing more than an ongoing and growing love relationship with God the Father, Son, and Holy Spirit."[18] Prayer is how we communicate with God—listening to His words, sharing our thoughts, hearing His heart. And this process of communication deepens our devotion by promoting honesty, caring, and understanding. There are many types of prayer—petitioning God for help, praising God, confessing sin, meditating on God's word. But all prayer works to draw us closer to God and increase our intimacy with Him.

The presence of the Holy Spirit in our lives enables prayer since we are connected to God through His indwelling in us. In Romans 8, the apostle Paul encourages his readers to recognize that they are children of God, not slaves living in fear. This spirit of sonship is confirmed in our lives by the presence of the Holy Spirit: "The Spirit himself testifies with our spirit that we are God's children."[19] Thus, prayer is not something we have to struggle to maintain or perform correctly. Instead, it is the simple flow of relationship between two people in love. And God Himself through the person of the Holy Spirit makes prayer work. As Foster notes, "Our prayer is to be like a reflex action to God's prior initiative upon the heart."[20]

The beautiful thing about prayer is that as we deepen our intimacy with God, we experience increasingly more of His love and affection. Some Christians are quick to discount feelings when it comes to our relationship with God. We are often warned against seeking emotional highs or living for mountaintop experiences. And certainly such experiences alone should never be our end goal. Our goal is devotion to God. But our devotion to God is strengthened when we experience Him. As we feel His nearness, hear His voice, and enjoy His love, we grow into stronger, deeper, more committed Christians. As the English novelist and essayist E. M. Forster once wrote, "Ecstasy doesn't last. But it cuts a channel for something lasting."[21] Prayer is one of our best avenues to growing in intimacy with God, and devotion increases dramatically when we experience Him in intimate, profound ways.

The church I grew up in did not emphasize experiencing God's presence in prayer. I had to learn how to still my spirit before the Lord so I could feel His nearness. Learning to calm my racing mind and unruly emotions took time, but God was patient with me, and I grew in learning to rest in God's presence. One promise from a book on prayer I read at the time helped me immeasurably: "Whenever we yearn to make a fresh start in our relationship with God, the place to begin is with the realization that the desire is, of itself, God's work. There is no need for us to struggle back to some spiritual starting line before we start to pray again. God chalks the starting line just where we are."[22] I loved that picture of God meeting us right where we are, chalking the starting line so we can begin to move forward.

If your prayer life is not what you would like it to be, the reminder that God is the One who initiates relationship with us should serve to encourage you. Remember, Moses didn't set the bush on fire to find God. You don't have to struggle to make prayer "work;" instead, start by simply committing to spending ten to fifteen minutes a day in God's presence and ask Him to meet you. God wants to draw closer to us in prayer, so use your time with Him to talk out things that are on your mind, think deeply about a Bible verse, listen for His voice, or rest quietly in His presence. With practice, those precious minutes will become times of real communication between God and yourself, and those moments of sharing will increase your devotion to the One who loves you and cares for your soul.

4: FASTING

A final way to increase devotion that we learn from Anna is fasting. Luke mentions that fasting is a regular part of Anna's lifestyle. While we can fast from anything in our lives, such as television, gossiping, or unhealthy habits, fasting from food is the most common means of fasting in the Bible.[23] It is a practice that requires that we forgo our natural desire to eat for a determined period. Christian fasting is based in part on Jesus' answer to the disciples of John the Baptist when they came to Him with a question about fasting. In Matthew 9:15,

Jesus reveals that He expected His followers to fast after His ascension to the Father: "How can the guests of the bridegroom mourn while he is with them? The time will come when the bridegroom will be taken from them; then they will fast." Clearly, we are in the time now of Jesus' physical absence from the world, so fasting should be a discipline that we practice.

However, fasting has fallen on hard times in the western Christian world, and few practice the discipline. This is regrettable, as many benefits can come from fasting. In terms of increasing devotion, fasting is a helpful tool. Fasting often reveals what controls us, as going without food will challenge anyone's good nature and normal defense mechanisms. Also, fasting reminds us that we are sustained solely by God, dependent on Him for even our daily life and sustenance. Fasting also helps us keep our lives in balance. Hunger pains remind us of the relative insignificance of life's nonessentials.

Most importantly, however, fasting increases our personal devotion to God because fasting requires us to voluntarily choose to place ourselves in a position of weakness and need. Through fasting, we willingly diminish our strength and choose to experience lack. This is not our usual instinct! We are wired instead to use any means available to meet our needs and maintain a place of strength regardless of cost. Instead, when we fast, we declare to God that we are willing to inhabit a place of weakness in order that He might further His purposes for us and for the world. That is why fasting is so often connected in Scripture to prayer. In this place of submission and vulnerability, our love and devotion to the Lord grows and our hearts learn to trust in Him alone. Skipping lunch and spending that hour in prayer, forgoing dessert or sweets for a time, or even fasting regularly one day per week can work into our lives a consistent reminder of the eternal care of our heavenly Father and our own insufficiency. When we willingly relinquish our power, we draw closer to the One who holds all power and uses that sovereignty for our growth and good. This increased trust in God deepens devotion.

THE FRUITS OF DEVOTION

John Woolman was a local businessman and lay Christian minister who lived in Philadelphia during the late eighteenth century. Woolman's life is known to us today through his personal journal, which he kept intermittently from the time he was thirty-six years old until his death at the age of fifty-two. Known for his sincere devotion to God, Woolman was unique in his time for evidencing a rather modern commitment to the poor and marginalized. Woolman refused to use his trade business to trap consumers in debt, he would not use dyes or sugar because they were produced by slave labor, he fought for the abolition of all racial slavery in the colonies, and he championed the rights of

Native Americans, leading one modern philosopher to call Woolman the "first Apostle of human freedom."[24] During his lifetime, Woolman enjoyed a fruitful ministry throughout his region and believed that his power to minister came directly from his personal experiences with the Lord. According to Woolman, when we are called to minister to someone, we are "called to minister of that which [we] have tasted and handled spiritually."[25]

Devotion allows us to "taste" and "handle" the things of God. It connects us to the Father in a way that is powerful and transformative. As we progress in devotion, our passion for God increases and we experience more of His fruit in our lives. One fruit of Anna's devotion to God is that she receives her heart's desire: God Himself, the One to whom she has devoted her life, comes to her personally in the form of the infant Jesus. Although Anna is a marginalized widow who is barred from entering the inner court of the temple, Anna encounters the Lord. She witnesses the One who will bring abundant life and remove the power of discontentment. She greets the One who will break off all spiritual and human restrictions and open the path to God. She touches the One who is the Desire of the Nations, the One who will redeem Israel and all the world from sin and death. And, most importantly, she is honored to recognize God's Chosen One when many others do not because, as we noted above in Psalm 50:23, her devotion opens the way for her to receive the revelation of "the salvation of God."

What is your heart's desire? If, like Anna, our devotion is for God Himself, we will be blessed to "taste" and "handle" the sweet presence of God, and our hearts will be content. Our longings for the things of this world will fade as we encounter the living God, and the desires of our hearts will be satisfied.

But Anna enjoys a second fruit of devotion and that is the opportunity to be a blessing to other people. Luke tells us that Anna speaks prophetically over Jesus and provides encouragement to those who were waiting for God's salvation. When we live lives of devotion to God, not only do we move beyond our boundaries and receive the desires of our hearts, but others experience the overflow of what we have "tasted" and "handled." Our intimacy with God spills over into the lives of those around us, providing them with encouragement and even direction. Those who were in the temple that day surely experienced renewed hope for Israel. Luke tells us in verse 33 that Joseph and Mary "marveled" at the words shared about their Son. Being used by God to transform the lives around us is another blessing of devotion.

I have found that often during my own prayer time, someone else's concern will come to mind and God will give me direction on how to pray for that person. Sometimes, I have not even known the circumstances of the person I was praying for, but followed God's direction on how to pray. One time, God led me to pray specifically that a friend of mine would have the courage to move forward into a new prospect the Lord had for her. When I shared this with my friend, she gasped because she had been asking the Lord whether she should move forward into the new opportunity she believed God had placed before her. I knew nothing of this new opportunity for my friend, but I knew enough to obey God's prompting in prayer, and thus experienced an overflow of my devotion to the Lord in the form of a prayer request and timely word for someone I cared about. Ministry that overflows from our devotion to God will not always be earth-shattering, but it will be valuable in blessing others.

Lastly, Anna's devotion to God earns her a place of honor among the followers of God. She is immortalized in Scripture as a symbol of what all of Israel should have been at the time of God's visitation. The longing of the Father was for all His people to recognize and value His Son, but, sadly, most Israelites did not. Anna stands as a representation of what God hoped for at the time and still desires in His followers—people with hearts that are so attuned to God's heart that they recognize His hand wherever it appears and they value and acknowledge it. You will notice that as your passion for God increases through devotion to Him, you will be recognized among Christians and non-Christians as a person who knows God and desires Him. Your life and ministry will evidence the effects of a life devoted to the one true God, and His majesty, beauty, and power will be manifested through your life.

As we cultivate true devotion to God, our spiritual passion will have a firm foundation on which to grow, and we will move beyond the boundaries and discontentment that often threaten our joy. Like the maiden in the Song of Songs, we will be like a garden open only to the Lord, a fertile vineyard that enjoys God's care and love. As God says to His people through the prophet Isaiah:

Sing about a fruitful vineyard:
I, the Lord watch over it;
I water it continually.
I guard it day and night
so that no one may harm it.[26]

Devotion will provide the foundation for our passionate pursuit of the Lord, and we will evidence the love and intimacy that God desires with each believer.

02: COURAGE

FACING FEAR

When I was young, I fancied myself a gifted short story writer. Like my other dream of becoming a famous pop star, this one did not pan out for me, but those hours spent singing into my Shaun Cassidy karaoke machine or composing spine-tingling short stories late into the night *did* keep me from engaging in more sinister adolescent activities. And my short story efforts also gave me an abundance of material to read to my children at bedtime years later. One story, however, that I never dared read to them was my thriller titled "Fear." In this one-page, double-spaced masterpiece, the main character experiences paroxysms of terror because of sounds he hears behind him on a dark street. In the end, however, it is revealed that his imagination has been playing tricks on him, and the street is empty. In my youthful attempt at the sublime, I ended my story with the warning: "He had nothing to fear, but fear itself!" Hmmm . . . can't imagine where I got that line.

Fear is an obstacle that we all encounter, regardless of our age, gender, education, or socioeconomic status. It can creep in to ruin our fun at the most unsuspected times, changing our mood and virtually paralyzing us with anxiety and uncertainty. In Virginia Woolf's novel *To the Lighthouse*, matronly Mrs. Ramsey is spending an enjoyable afternoon with friends and family at her beach house, her youngest son James playing quietly on her lap, when she is suddenly startled by the realization that her children are growing up. At once, the familiar parental fears accost her. How will they fare in life, she wonders. Will they be safe and happy? Will they succeed? Woolf presents Mrs. Ramsey's sudden encounter with fear as a battle with life itself:

> She took a look at life, for she had a clear sense of it there . . . . A sort of transaction went on between them, in which she was on one side, and life was on another, and she was always trying to get the better of it, as it was of her; and sometimes they parleyed (when she sat alone); there were, she remembered, great reconciliation scenes; but for the most part, oddly enough, she must admit that she felt this thing that she called life terrible, hostile, and quick to pounce on you if you gave it a chance.[1]

Fear can give us the feeling that life is out to get us.

Mrs. Ramsey's sudden descent into fear would be described by psychologists today as "catastrophizing." Catastrophizing has been defined as "a process of exaggerated worrying, helpless, and distress-amplifying thoughts" which can spill over into all areas of our lives.[2] I've always used the term "snowballing" because, in the same way that a snowball gathers snow and grows in size as it rolls down a hill, so my fears can sometimes grow exponentially, moving from manageable to paralyzing with lightning speed. One minute I have a headache, and the next minute I'm certain I'm dying of an inoperable brain tumor. And I don't think I'm alone in my ability to catastrophize. Our society seems to have a pervasive struggle with the often debilitating effects of fear and anxiety.

As Christians, we recognize that fear can sidetrack our efforts to grow in our passion for God. One problem with fear is the ripple effect it creates. When we live with the belief that life is arrayed against us, everything in our life suffers. We worry about both the present and the future, we doubt our own strength and abilities, and we may even question God's love and care for us. Our sleep may be affected, our health can suffer, and we may even choose to abandon long-cherished dreams and desires because of our apprehension. Worse, our relationships with others suffer as well, as we respond to them from a position of anxiety rather than serenity. We may experience jealousy in friendships, exhibit overprotectiveness in family relationships, or hesitate to form new relationships. Fear can be one of the most effective and destructive weapons of the enemy of our souls because of its far-reaching consequences.

But fear also can undermine our relationship with God. In chapter 4 of 1 John, the apostle John reminds his readers that their relationship with God is based on God's love, and then encourages them to love each other as a reflection of this same love. Several verses later, John makes an interesting remark: "There is no fear in love. But perfect love drives out fear, because fear has to do with punishment. The one who fears is not made perfect in love."[3] Why are fear and love presented as mutually exclusive in this passage? Would we not expect to see love contrasted with hate, perhaps, or anger? What is it about fear that makes it unable to coexist with love?

I believe one answer lies in the distraction that fear presents. When we fear something or someone, our focus immediately moves to what we fear. We obsess about it, we conjure up ways to combat it, we talk to others incessantly about it. Thus, the object of our fear effectively achieves the central place in our lives, moving our focus off where it should be: God. Just as the disciple Peter began to sink in the water as he took his eyes off Jesus in Matthew 14, so fear shifts our focus and directs our efforts and attention away from God, and the object of our fear fills our world. Like fear, however, love is supremely engaging, and just as able to fill our world. As when we are with someone we love, nothing else matters. So love, with its drawing power, can effectively remove our attention from the object of our fear and center it instead on the one we love. And if the one we love is God, we enjoy the even more enviable position of perfect peace and rest based on God's love and power, which are without fault and without limit. So the perfect love of God does drive out fear as the two cannot coexist in the human heart.

In 2 Kings 4, we read the story of a woman who is in an extremely fearful situation. Her husband, a local prophet in Israel, has died, and she is left alone with her two sons. Sadly, not only must she grieve the loss of her husband and the companionship, status, and security that he provided, but she also faces perhaps an even more difficult situation—significant debt. Without a means to pay the debt, she is left awaiting the creditor who is coming to take her two sons as slaves for payment. This widow's situation provides her with much to be fearful about as she is on the brink of losing everyone she loves. Worse yet, she does not have many resources or options and must confront her daunting future alone.

Most of us can empathize with the widow, as we all encounter situations that cause us fear. What is currently gnawing at your sense of peace and security? Fear of losing your job? Financial stress? Marriage issues that appear irreconcilable? Children who appear headed in the wrong direction? An elderly parent, a suspicious lump, a leaky roof, an unwise business investment? Our minds know no bounds when it comes to conjuring up worst-case scenarios. And many of our worries are legitimate. But we don't have to live constantly worrying about what is around the next corner. As children of the God of the universe, we can embrace Jesus' promise in John 16:33b: "In this world you will have trouble. But take heart! I have overcome the world." Jesus doesn't guarantee that we will escape all of life's difficulties, but He does declare that His authority over all creation should encourage and reassure us when we face frightening circumstances. How can we embrace Jesus' promise and move forward confidently in the face of fear?

ANTIDOTE TO FEAR: COURAGE

The component of a passionate Christian life that can overcome fear is courage. Courage is seldom discussed in Christian circles, and its role in the believer's life is tragically underestimated. Pursuing the kingdom of God requires the bravery to deal with the fear that comes from setbacks, uncertainty, opposition, and our own self-doubt. Following Jesus is not for the faint of heart.

Courage is key to spiritual passion because it is an antidote to fear and can move us beyond our panic and anxieties. When we press forward regardless of the circumstances and our own misgivings, we find that Franklin Delano Roosevelt's words during his first inaugural address as President of the United States are true: "The only thing we have to fear is fear itself." In his speech,

Roosevelt exposes the true nature of fear, calling it an "unreasoning, unjustified terror which paralyzes needed efforts to convert retreat into advance."[4] Roosevelt spoke those words during a time of great panic in America as the Great Depression showed no signs of abating and the country was gripped by hopelessness and an unemployment rate of approximately thirty-three percent. Yet, by implementing new government programs under his New Deal such as the Agricultural Adjustment Act of 1933 and the Works Progress Administration, Roosevelt was able to lead Americans on a new path forward. By 1934, unemployment relief was flowing to workers in all parts of the country; in some areas, as much as forty percent of the population was receiving aid.[5]

Roosevelt's words are true—courage is necessary to "convert retreat into advance," in the spiritual life as well as the physical. Think of the last time you failed to walk in obedience to God's word. Was it lack of effort or ability that held you back, or simply fear? Sometimes growing as a Christian doesn't require wisdom or gifting or maturity; it takes a simple gritting of our teeth and moving forward despite our fears. As beatnik writer Ambrose Redmoon once observed:

> Courage is not the absence of fear, but rather the judgment that something else is more important than one's fear. The timid presume it is lack of fear that allows the brave to act when the timid do not. But to take action when one is not afraid is easy. To refrain when afraid is also easy. To take action regardless of fear is brave.[6]

Fear will paralyze us and stop all forward progress, but courage releases us to move forward and engage, developing and growing as a passionate follower of Jesus in the process.

When I began writing my first book, I started with a sense of mission and confidence. I committed time to writing, fitting it in around teaching and raising two boys. I hoped the book would be written quickly and that publishers would jump at the chance to print it. As the years and the revisions dragged on, and the manuscript was rejected by press after press, my confidence began to turn into fear that the book would never be accepted for publication. When I began the project, I believed in my heart that God would help me see it through to completion, but eventually my eyes drifted from God to the stack of rejection letters steadily growing on my desk.

One day, as I sat down to revise the manuscript, I mumbled to myself, "I don't know why I do this; nothing is going to come of all this work." Suddenly, I felt conviction from the Holy Spirit in my heart. What was I saying? Quite simply, fear of failure was consuming me. At that instant, I changed my attitude. From then on, every time doubt came into my heart I pushed it away, "taking every thought captive," as Paul encourages his readers to do in 2 Corinthians 10:5

(NASB). I had no guarantee of commercial success, but I knew what God had called me to do at that time, and that was to write a book. The final revision took almost two years to complete, but in the end it was published. Demonstrating courage in the spiritual life certainly does not mean that everything will always go our way, but it does help us "convert retreat into advance," keeping us moving forward and allowing opportunities for God to work in our lives.

In our story, the widow decides to "advance" before the creditor comes to take her sons into slavery, by seeking out the prophet Elisha and asking him what to do. His response surely surprised her:

> Elisha replied to her, "How can I help you? Tell me, what do you have in your house?"
>
> "Your servant has nothing there at all," she said, "except a small jar of olive oil."
>
> Elisha said, "Go around and ask all your neighbors for empty jars. Don't ask for just a few. Then go inside and shut the door behind you and your sons. Pour oil into all the jars, and as each is filled, put it to one side."[7]

The widow does as Elisha suggests, borrowing jars from her neighbors and filling each jar with oil from her small supply. Miraculously, the oil does not run out until the last jar is filled. When she returns to Elisha to tell him what occurred, the prophet replies, "Go, sell the oil and pay your debts. You and your sons can live on what is left."[8] This widow's courage saved her two sons from slavery and provided the entire family with a secure future. Acting with courage is never easy, but this mother made important choices that reflect a willingness to move forward despite the fear she was certainly feeling. Let's examine the brave choices she made.

CHOOSING COURAGE

The first aspect of courage that the widow reveals is a willingness to take the first step. When Elisha asks her what she has in her house, she offers her small jar of olive oil. Certainly, she knew that one small jar of oil could not pay off her debts, but she offered it to the prophet nonetheless, as it was all that she possessed. Courage begins with a willingness to step out in faith with what we have, not wait until we are more prepared, more mature, more certain of the outcome, or more confident. When courage is required, we will always feel less than fully prepared, less than fully mature, less than certain of the outcome, and less than completely confident. It is the brave person who moves forward despite these feelings.

It is a sometimes perplexing reality that in the economy of God's kingdom, what we receive can depend on what we already have and are willing to use. In the parable of the talents, Jesus tells of a master who takes a journey and leaves his wealth in the care of his servants. To one servant he gives five bags of gold, to another two bags, and to another one bag. While he is gone, the first two servants put their money to work and double the funds with which they have been entrusted. The servant with one bag, however, buries his bag to keep it safe. When the master returns, he rewards each of the first two servants with these words: "Well done, good and faithful servant! You have been faithful with a few things; I will put you in charge of many things." Then the last servant proudly returns his bag of gold to his master, remarking that he was "afraid [to lose the money] and went out and hid your gold in the ground." The master retorts that at least he could have put the money in the bank to gain interest and angrily gives the bag of gold to the first servant, sending the last servant out of his presence and into the darkness. The parable ends with the message, "For whoever has will be given more, and they will have an abundance. Whoever does not have, even what they have will be taken from them."[9] What is interesting in this passage is that the first two servants both receive the same commendation from the master, even though one servant was entrusted with more of the master's wealth. What they have in common is a willingness to take the first step and use what they have, regardless of their fear or the number of their resources. On the other hand, the last servant is not condemned for having less gold than the others, but for allowing fear to paralyze him. As the parable implies, God's blessing comes as we step out bravely and use what He has already given us.

Taking the first step is easier when we take the time to recognize the resources that are right in front of us. Do you have friends who can offer support and encouragement in a time of anxiety? Call them. Have you experienced a similarly fearful situation in which God delivered you? Recall it to mind continually and remember his faithfulness. Can you pay off a fraction of what you owe to creditors, offer one small compliment to the person you are struggling with, make one counseling appointment to begin the healing process, register for one class at the local community college? If we desire to move forward into a passionate spiritual life, we must remember that courage does not mean accomplishing the entire daunting task before us at once; it means using what we have to take the *first step*.

The second important choice that the widow makes is to trust and obey the words of Elisha. Her confidence in the word of God fuels her courage, and she displays faith that God can and will help her. Courage is bolstered when we believe in God's goodness and power. As God promises us in Jeremiah 29:11, he has "plans to prosper you and not to harm you, plans to give you hope and a future." Trusting that God loves us and will help us is crucial to developing courage.

But often our faith is weak, and we just can't seem to kindle the trust in God that we need. This is when obedience can bridge the gap. When we choose to obey God even without much faith, our courage is strengthened. The widow demonstrates obedience to God's word when she follows the prophet's advice and collects jars from her neighbors. As readers of the story, we might be tempted to think that it does not take much courage on the part of the widow to obey the prophet's instructions. But consider what this mother has to choose *not* to do if she is to use her precious time to collect jars. If she decides to follow Elisha's somewhat strange instructions, she will have to forgo other actions that probably make more sense to her and seemingly offer a greater chance of success. Should she use the precious time before the creditor's arrival to collect jars, or should she travel to her wealthy uncle's house to ask for a loan? Should she perhaps use the valuable time to beg at the city gate in an attempt to raise the money? Talk to the chief priests or call in some favors from her husband's connections as a local prophet? We do not know what potential solutions the widow has to sacrifice in order to follow Elisha's directives, but we do know that she chooses to obey the man of God rather than act on her own solutions. Is there a challenge in your life that requires courage, but you are struggling with trusting God enough to move forward? Try obedience. Then see if your trust in God, and consequently your courage, grow as a result. Courage is strengthened when trust and obedience work together to propel us forward on God's path, despite our doubts and uncertainties.

After taking the first step and then moving forward with trust and obedience, the widow makes a third choice that reinforces her courage—she displays a total commitment to the path she has chosen to follow. She and her sons do not play it safe and collect just a few jars—they gather as many jars as they can. When God calls us to step out with courage, we must go all the way. Halfway commitments usually end in disappointment or failure. In one episode of the television show *Nikita*, a former secret agent struggles to explain to her friend why she was ultimately successful in dismantling an evil government program. Nikita finally says, "In that time, no one thought I could be stopped because they thought I was stronger, faster. It had nothing to do with that . . . . I was committed. I was more committed than my enemies. I believed."[10] Even if we are not secret agents, God promises us in 2 Corinthians 9:6 that whoever "sows generously will also reap generously." The more we pour into God's kingdom, the more results we will see. This assurance comes not from our own abilities, but from the reality that God works through us. Paul continues in the passage to affirm this: "And God is able to bless you abundantly, so that in all things at all times, having all that you need, you will abound in every good work."[11] If God has placed something before you to do, do not play it safe—pursue it with total commitment as the widow did.

Lastly, the widow makes a choice that we might not naturally associate with bravery—she accepts interdependence. The widow's success was dependent on her neighbors' resources and willingness to help her by lending her jars. Although courage is often presented to us as a solitary attribute, as Christians, we know that we are designed to work with other people, particularly believers. When we are struggling to move forward with courage, others can lift us up and encourage us, offering us their own resources as we have need. Just as Aaron and Hur physically upheld Moses' arms during the battle with the Amalekites in Exodus 17 to release the power of God on behalf of the Israelite army, so our brothers and sisters can sustain us during times when we are struggling to be brave. If we are resistant to that help, we can miss out on the opportunity for our courage to grow.

A few years ago, over a six-month period, I experienced my father's unexpected passing, my grandmother's sudden decline and death, and a close family member's diagnosis of cancer and subsequent surgery. That this all transpired three thousand miles from where I lived added an additional layer of stress as I attempted to support and guide my mother through this fearful and painful time while processing my own emotions and collecting more frequent flyer miles than I could use in a lifetime. Through the wonders of electronic communication, however, I never felt alone, as my friends, family, and prayer partners were constantly in touch with me, supporting and encouraging me. I actually ended up with carpal tunnel-like symptoms from texting so much during those months! Beyond emotional support, my friends also helped my husband keep the household running while I traveled to be with my family. If you had asked me before that time how I would expect to fare in such a situation, I would never have guessed the courage and strength I would find through the support and assistance of my friends. Like me, the widow certainly receives strength and courage from her neighbors as she moves toward God's miraculous provision for her. Those of us who have experienced the help of others during a fearful or difficult experience know that courage is strengthened when we are supported by those who care.

THE EFFECTS OF COURAGE

The widow enjoys immediate fruit from her act of courage. I would imagine that the first emotion she experiences when she begins pouring oil into one jar after another is hope. For the first time, she can envision a way out of her terrifying circumstances. Fear can cause despair and hopelessness when it seems there is no escape from our situation. But courage is proactive, so it moves our hearts from dejection to expectation. As my childhood pastor loved to remind us, God guides a moving object. When we take that courageous first step, God can work with us to open doors we never thought possible. Consider it godly "snowballing," as our faith gains momentum through the hope that comes when we step out in courage.

Besides simply hope, the widow experiences provision from God when she acts bravely. In fact, she gets to witness a miracle! Through the multiplying flow of the oil, God provides for her and for her family, giving her enough to pay off her debts and save her sons from slavery. Her needs are amply supplied by God, who always does "immeasurably more than all we ask or imagine."[12]

But, more than simply providing for the widow's current needs, God goes above and beyond to actually restore her to the place of security and strength that she lost upon her husband's death. Before her act of bravery, the widow was in a position of weakness: no income, no status, no prospects, no security, no hope. Now, the abundance she receives from the Lord restores her family to a position of safety and strength, as she has more resources than she currently needs. This is a beautiful truth about God—He always seeks not only to meet our existing needs, but also to restore to us what was lost. Through His presence and power in our lives, He works to "bestow on [believers] a crown of beauty instead of ashes, the oil of joy instead of mourning, and a garment of praise instead of a spirit of despair."[13] Although perfect restoration will ultimately be accomplished only at the end of time, God's plan of restoration was set in motion immediately after the Fall with the promise of Jesus. God wants to restore His people—He desires that we be whole, strong, hopeful, and joyful—and He is working toward that goal now. Whatever we have experienced as loss or pain may not be *replaced*, but it can be *restored* by God as He heals and strengthens us. The widow's courage during her time of loss and fear allows God to restore her family to a place of stability and hope for the future.

A friend of mine leads a ministry to those trapped in sex trafficking in the city of Los Angeles, California. God's promise in Isaiah 61 to restore to His people a "crown of beauty instead of ashes" is a key verse for this ministry as their mission is to see beautiful, beloved children of God brought out of their painful circumstances and into an intimate, healing relationship with their Creator and Father. Such ministry requires great courage, as many of the men and women are caught in complex webs of addiction, codependence, profound hopelessness, and lack of resources. Yet, despite these obstacles, many are being reached for Christ and offered a way out of their emptiness and despair. In a recent ministry update, my friend shared this story of God's work:

> You have been praying for C for several months now. Last week she made the choice to get off the streets and start a new life. She is doing really well! One thing that really encouraged me is that when she thought of

who her friends were that she could call for support, she thought of us. C had always held us at arm's length and it was hard to tell if we were having any sort of impact. Praise God for His faithfulness; He truly does bring the increase.

Without God's promises of restoration through His power and love, my friend would have nothing to offer these men and women who so desperately need to know that a loving God desires to heal and restore them. God's power to restore offers hope to many as my friend and her coworkers move forward with courage and faith.

A final fruit of courage experienced by the widow is a personal experience that produces a testimony. When we have an encounter with the Lord, we are left with a story to tell—to ourselves and to others. The widow may have been taught from childhood that God would provide for all her needs, but now she has miraculously experienced that provision, and her own life will never be the same. As Job remarked after his intense personal encounter with God: "I had only heard about you before, but now I have seen you with my own eyes. I take back everything I said, and I sit in dust and ashes to show my repentance."[14] What Job knew in his head to be true about God became more real to him through a personal encounter. Like Job, the widow now has a personal experience that will encourage her when she is faced with fearful situations in the future. Stepping out in courage places us in a position to encounter God in a life-changing way.

But the nature of testimony is that it is shared, and I find it hard to imagine that the widow kept the news of the miracle that God had performed to herself. By sharing her story of God's faithfulness and provision with those in her town, she undoubtedly became an encouragement and example to her entire village of God as Yahweh Yireh—the God who Provides. And just think of the impact of her courage on her sons! In the aftermath of their own father's death, her children have now experienced for themselves the power and loving care of their heavenly Father. The words of Psalm 78 reflect the power of testimony through generations: "We will tell the next generation the praiseworthy deeds of the Lord, his power, and the wonders he has done.... Then they would put their trust in God and would not forget his deeds but would keep his commands."[15] An encounter with God always gives us a testimony that will encourage and bless all who hear it.

Fear is one of the enemy's greatest weapons, and it seems to be rampant in our society today. As Christians, we can make the choice for courage, even when everything seems to be against us. The choice to be brave and move forward is part of a passionate Christian life and is not based on our own gumption, but rather on God's promises to us in Scripture—such as the one found in Proverbs 3:25–26:

Have no fear of sudden disaster
or of the ruin that overtakes the wicked,
for the Lord will be at your side
and will keep your foot from being snared.

We know that the God of all power, authority, and kindness will be at our side, and we can rely on His goodness and love to see us through even the darkest and most disastrous of times.

03: FAITH

DEFEATING DOUBT

Would you like to be a princess? Live in a castle, wear beautiful gowns, be attended to by a gaggle of servants, and have your face on your country's currency? Sounds like a pretty good gig. But what about being a princess *and* then a queen? Now that would be the perfect fairy tale! Know anyone with a life like that?

Michal enjoyed just such a life, and her story appears in the pages of the Old Testament books of 1 and 2 Samuel. Born a princess under the reign of her father King Saul, she becomes attracted to David, a shepherd boy selected by God to succeed her father after Saul's heart turns cold toward the Lord. After marrying David, Michal appears destined for an effortless shift from princess to queen; however, the young couple's future together becomes complicated by Saul's desire to hold on to the throne and the long, difficult road David must travel to finally become king. Michal's life is an example of a woman given an opportunity to exercise faith and believe God's promises in the midst of challenging times. And, as we might expect, Michal experiences a mixture of both success and failure.

As modern believers who are seeking to grow in our zeal for the Lord, we must grow in faith because, quite simply, a passionate Christian life requires it. Lots of it. Setbacks, disappointments, surprises, detours—they are a part of life for every believer. To maintain our passion for God and His purposes, we need faith. As the apostle Paul reminds us in 2 Corinthians, faith enables us to maintain our passion despite stressful, painful circumstances:

> We are hard pressed on every side, but not crushed; perplexed, but not in despair; persecuted, but not abandoned; struck down, but not destroyed .... It is written: "I believed; therefore I have spoken." Since we have that same spirit of faith, we also believe and therefore speak, because we know that the one who raised the Lord Jesus from the dead will also raise us with Jesus and present us with you to himself.[1]

Faith can help us move forward with passion, regardless of the circumstances facing us, by providing that spark we need to maintain hope. Faith can move mountains, according to Jesus in Matthew 21:21, because it motivates and sustains us in a way little else can.

I received a helpful reminder of the importance of faith from a young hotel manager in India named Sonny. Well, at least that's the character in the movie *The Best Exotic Marigold Hotel*. Trapped on a cross-country flight with nothing else to watch but this movie, I became instantly enamored of this twenty-something youngest son who believes he can make his family's dilapidated, out-of-fashion hotel a success by pitching it as a retirement inn to British seniors. His more successful brothers, part owners of the hotel along with Sonny, want to demolish the eyesore. Even Sonny's mother advises him to abandon the project, as well as his girlfriend of whom she disapproves, and return to Delhi for an arranged marriage. But Sonny ignores their naysaying and presses forward, buoyed by his seemingly blind faith that everything will work out. His consistent claim throughout the film is a supposed old Indian saying: "Everything will be all right in the end, so if it is not all right, it is not yet the end."[2] Of course, everything does work out all right in the end for Sonny and his friends, but even if we don't live in a Hollywood movie, we have Paul's reminder that a long-term perspective like Sonny's is part of being a follower of God: "Therefore we do not lose heart.... So we fix our eyes not on what is seen, but on what is unseen, since what is seen is temporary, but what is unseen is eternal."[3] Faith helps us move forward in passionate pursuit of God and His promises because we know God has good plans for us regardless of how our current circumstances may appear.

But what is faith, really? How can we define it? In Hebrews 11:1, Paul describes faith as "confidence in what we hope for and assurance about what we do not see." Faith is believing something that cannot be verified by our senses. I cannot see or measure my husband's love for me, but I believe him when he says he loves me. I cannot guarantee that my friend will show up for our scheduled lunch, but I drive to the restaurant expecting to meet her. I cannot make rain fall from the sky, but I throw an umbrella in my car when the weather channel tells me to expect precipitation. Faith is, as Paul says, a confidence that what we believe is true, regardless of whether we can empirically validate it. Our lives run on faith.

What, then, produces faith? I believe my husband because I know him well and trust his veracity. I show up to meet my friend because she has met me for countless lunches in the past. I grab my umbrella because the weather channel features trained meteorologists who have been right before. Faith is a combination of evaluation and memory. I evaluate the integrity of the person making the promise to me, and I recall instances in which the person has been true to his or her word.

The same approach holds true for my faith in God. I am in relationship with Him and have seen Him work in my life before, so I know Him and trust Him. I choose to believe in His goodness, His mercy, His power, and His love. I trust His promises to care for me and lead me, like the one in Romans 8:28: "And we know that in all things God works for the good of those who love Him, who have been called according to His purpose." I have staked my life and future on His trustworthiness, believing He is who He says He is and that He will be true to His word. My life in Him is one of faith. It's just that simple.

But, of course, it isn't *really* that simple, is it? Taking God at His word is something we all struggle with because we are human and because a fallen world often derails our best intentions. When we begin to lose our faith, we can come crashing directly into doubt. Doubt is the main obstacle to a life of faith because it causes us to lose our confidence in God and in what we believe. We may begin to doubt God's power to work in a situation, His willingness to help us, or even His very existence. We may question our relationship with Him, our ability to hear His voice, our strength to follow His commands. We may even doubt that He loves us. Suddenly, doubt takes over, and the beliefs we counted on before seem to dissipate into thin air, leaving us alone with only uncertainty. Passion for God and His purposes can easily evaporate in the face of paralyzing doubt.

So how can we develop a strong, vibrant faith that will help sustain a passionate spiritual life? Princess Michal offers us some clues to growing in faith. As a member of the royal family of Israel, Michal experiences many twists and turns in her life, sometimes exercising authentic faith and sometimes, unfortunately, failing to trust God. As we examine her life, we can learn from both her successes and failures as we strive to develop a strong faith for a passionate Christian life.

KEEP IN STEP WITH THE SPIRIT

Michal's early days with David show us three key steps to growing our faith. The first is to keep in step with the Spirit of God. When Michal meets David, he has already been secretly anointed as the next king of Israel and is serving King Saul as both a court musician and a military commander. David's success and popularity among the people are noted in 1 Samuel 18:7 as crowds are said to have proclaimed, "Saul has killed his thousands, but David his tens of thousands." Perhaps not surprisingly, father and daughter have opposing reactions to David—Saul becomes consumed with envy and hatred, while Michal desires to marry him.

Michal's choice of David as her life partner provides our first key in developing a strong faith—keeping in step with the Spirit, as Paul encourages us to do in Galatians 5:25.[4] By choosing to marry David, Michal makes the choice to align herself with the man to whom God has given His approval as well as the kingship, and she places herself squarely in the path of God's will for Israel. She thus removes herself from the rule of her father Saul, the king that God has rejected, and sides with David, the ruler chosen by God to bring His loving reign to Israel. While we are not given insight from the Scriptures into Michal's motivation for choosing David, we might surmise that she recognized in David a man who would be a king after God's own heart, instead of a selfish ruler like her father had become. That she chooses to love her father's competitor speaks to her own strength of personality and her willingness to make choices that she deems best. By choosing David, Michal keeps in step with the Spirit by leaving her father's rule and aligning with David, a ruler whose lineage will produce the long-awaited Messiah and last into perpetuity.

Regardless of what Michal's motivations were or weren't, we know that the benefit of keeping in step with the Spirit of God is that choosing God's way gives our faith a firm, trustworthy foundation. We find it easier to trust God because we know we are following His plan. Sometimes our understanding of God's intentions may be very specific, like clarity that God desires us to accept a certain job or marry a particular person. But sometimes this assurance is more general, like knowing God is working in our family, yet not being certain of exactly the outcome, or recognizing that God has brought a new friend into our lives to help us grow in an area of struggle, but not knowing specifically how that growth will happen. Either way, when we keep in step with God's Spirit, our faith has a solid foundation to sustain us when we face challenging times. When the job we accepted becomes challenging or the marriage we entered shows signs of strain, our faith is strengthened by our knowledge that we are in the path in which God's Spirit is moving.

But in order to make the choice to keep in step with the Spirit, we must be able to recognize the direction in which the Spirit is moving; otherwise, we are simply following our own impressions or desires. Recognizing how God is moving requires being able to hear God's voice and know His heart. How do we hear God's voice and know His heart? Spiritual practices such as reading and memorizing Scripture, attending to Bible-based teaching, living in fellowship with other believers who can speak into our lives, and learning to still our spirits in God's presence in prayer all enable us to hear Him and help us recognize how to align with Him. Learning how to hear God does not happen overnight, but it is the fruit of our growing intimacy with Jesus; as He promises us, "My sheep hear my voice, and I know them, and they follow me."[5]

ACT DECISIVELY

I haven't always been terribly successful at hearing God correctly, but part of growing in faith is learning to act decisively when we finally do tune in to what He is saying. My first plan for my life after college was to become a clinical psychologist. My entire undergraduate career was spent working toward this goal, so when I finally entered a Ph.D. program in clinical psychology upon graduation, I thought I was on my way to fulfilling my destiny. At the time, clinical psychology programs were more difficult to gain entrance into than even medical schools, so I was ecstatic to have squeaked into one. Imagine my distress when just a few months later, I began to have the sinking suspicion that I had made the wrong decision and that clinical psychology was not for me after all!

A call to my mom from my newly furnished apartment in Massachusetts gave me the answer I needed. She said to follow what I was hearing from God and not to be afraid to change course, even if it was a drastic step. That advice was what I needed to hear, and I left the program and headed home to Maryland, eventually enrolling in a graduate program in English the next semester. My father's reaction to moving all my belongings three hundred miles back home again only a few months after hauling them to my new apartment was also noteworthy, but not really printworthy. For a twenty-two-year-old, leaving that graduate program was a drastic move, but it taught me that decisive action is an important part of faith.

Michal finds she also must act decisively in the early days of her marriage to David. As King Saul's envy of David's military successes and popularity grows, the new bride experiences the shock of seeing her own father send a spear hurtling toward her husband in a rage. Eventually, Saul hatches a plot to kill David, stationing troops outside his house to capture him when he leaves the next morning. Michal gets wind of her father's plan and encourages David to sneak out of the house during the night. When the soldiers come to ask for David the next day, they are fooled by an idol that Michal has cleverly hidden in their bed, granting David precious lead time for his escape. By the time the soldiers discover the ruse, David has had quite a head start.[6] Michal's quick thinking saves David's life and highlights the second key in growing in faith—taking decisive action. Amidst certain emotional turmoil and fear, Michal takes a step of faith and saves the man she loves.

Faith cannot exist solely in the mind; it must find expression in action. When we truly believe in something, we will act on it. If I want a college education, I will register for classes. If I long to strengthen my relationship with God, I will begin memorizing Scripture. If I believe that God wants me to serve in the children's ministry at my church, I will sign up as a volunteer. As the New Testament author James reminds us, "You see that a person is considered righteous by what they do and not by faith alone .... As the body without the spirit is dead, so faith without deeds is dead."[7]

In addition to keeping in step with the Spirit, Michal evidences this second key of faith by acting on what she believes. According to 1 Samuel 19, Michal is the one who encourages David to leave before Saul's men can arrest him, helps him climb out a window, and distracts the soldiers with a decoy. Like choosing to follow her heart in selecting her father's competitor as her husband, Michal again acts decisively, even though she knows her choices will not please her father the king. She is bold and shrewd in her actions, and it is her faith and the actions that flow from it that save God's anointed king of Israel. When we act decisively, we give feet to our faith, and our trust in God has a concrete outcome.

TURN OVER THE DETAILS TO GOD

Decisive action that keeps in step with the Spirit must also be accompanied by a third key: giving the details to God. We must be content to play our role in God's plan, and then leave the rest to Him. If we do not, we risk trying to control more than what God has given us authority over. Michal follows God's lead to save David's life, but she cannot single-handedly accomplish a *coup d'état* for her husband and make him king. Instead, she releases David to God's care in the wilderness and gives herself to God's protection in the court of her now angry, betrayed father.

Releasing to God what we are not called to control is a key part of faith because it enables us to participate with God and follow His lead, but also leaves room for God to work as He pleases, perhaps using situations and people that we never would have considered. Think back to a recent situation in your life that God resolved in a way you did not expect. Could the resolution have happened if you had attempted to handle every detail of the situation yourself? Probably not. Attempting to control each and every aspect of a situation is less about faith and more about selfishness. A healthy faith strengthens us to act decisively, but also to keep our focus on the role God has called us to play in His Story.

Those of us who are parents must learn this lesson early in our child's life, or we are in for a long, rocky road. While we are called by God to train our children in godliness, protect them from danger, and encourage them to become all that God has made them to be, we cannot save them from every painful circumstance or do everything for them if we want them to mature. As our children grow into adulthood, we must turn over more and more to the Lord, yet still act decisively as godly parents when called to do so. Leaving my older son crying in his kindergarten class, making him stay on the losing baseball team through the end of the season, and watching him drive off by himself to school only one day after receiving his driver's license have all been opportunities for me to act in my child's best interest and then release the rest to God in faith.

Although releasing the details of a situation or relationship to God is important for faith, doing so often can be extremely difficult or, at times, seemingly impossible. While many spiritual practices will help us in these times, I have found that remembering and declaring God's truth is the most effective way for me to let go of the details and give my fears to Him. When I recall the reality of God's mercy, love, power, and authority and declare my belief in those truths (sometimes fifty times a day!), trusting Him with the little things becomes easier. Let me tell you a story to illustrate my point. A talented singer-songwrit-er—hand-picked by the senior pastor of a large, influential church—enjoyed his life of ministering to the Lord in music and song. He was respected and admired for his ability to draw others into the presence of God. As his ministry grew over the years, however, he found himself struggling with deep questions about the unfairness of life. Why did evil people prosper while many good, upright people suffered? Why did so many mock and disobey God seemingly without reper-cussions? Did his devotion and obedience to God count for nothing? He became so obsessed with the inequity he saw in the world that he became bitter and grieved in his spirit, unable to trust God with the injustice he saw in the world.

Thankfully, our troubled worship leader remembered the way to strengthen his waning faith—he entered God's sanctuary, the place of His presence, and meditated on God's truth. There, he recalled and declared the absolute certainty of God's righteous judgments and the sad destiny of those who reject Him. In his own words:

> When I tried to understand all this,
> it troubled me deeply
> till I entered the sanctuary of God;
> then I understood their final destiny.[8]

The musician acknowledged the beautiful reality of life with God: "Yet I am al-ways with you; you hold me by my right hand. You guide me with your counsel, and afterward you will take me into glory."[9] Do you recognize this person? It is the Old Testament psalmist Asaph, and I've slightly modernized his experi-ence as it appears in Psalm 73. Remembering and declaring God's truth did not answer every question for Asaph, nor did it help him unravel every specific situation that had disturbed him, but it changed him, encouraged him, and re-oriented him so that he could release the ultimate details of his life to God. It buoyed His faith. God's truth always brings freedom for the believer—in this case, freedom to help us release control and trust God.

We have observed three important keys to a life of passionate faith—keep in step with the Spirit of God, take action, and turn over the details to God. Michal seems to use these strategies to maintain her faith in God and His promis-es while her father's envy threatened her future. Unfortunately, this is where Michal's life of faith appears to end. The next time we see our princess, she ap-pears to have lost her once robust, passionate faith. What can we learn from her failure to trust God and move forward in faith?

MICHAL'S LOSS OF FAITH

If you are familiar with Michal and David's story, you know that they ultimately are reunited and that David, at the age of almost thirty-eight, is finally made king of all Israel.[10] Michal is now a queen and God's promises have been fulfilled, but Michal has suffered much along the way. During the years of David's exile, Michal endured her father's tortured, obsessive pursuit of David; was married off by her father to another man as an act of revenge; and experienced David's choice to take additional wives during his time as a fugitive. Much of what Michal had hoped for in her life has been destroyed by painful, cold realities.

We rejoin Michal in 2 Samuel 6 as King David decides to celebrate all that the Lord has done by bringing to Jerusalem the Ark of the Covenant, the chest in which the Ten Commandments are kept and a central symbol for all Israel that God is with them. Bringing the ark to Jerusalem is a historic moment for the people, and they celebrate the Lord's unification of their nation under David with animal sacrifices, music, and triumphant dancing. David himself joins the people and dances before the Lord "with all his might," clothed only in a snug, sleeveless linen garment worn by the priests.[11]

But Michal is not celebrating. In fact, she is not even among the procession; she is alone in her room, watching the festivities from above and, according to 2 Samuel 6:16, "despis[ing]" the celebratory dancing of her husband. When David returns home that evening, eager to share his joy with his family, Michal sarcastically upbraids him with the words, "How the king of Israel has distinguished himself today, going around half-naked in full view of the slave girls of his servants as any vulgar fellow would!"[12] Undeterred, David defends his worship of God, claiming, "I will celebrate before the Lord. I will become even more undignified than this, and I will be humiliated in my own eyes."[13] David is willing to set aside his own "dignity" and worship God for what He has done, while Michal cannot enter into the joy of the people of Israel nor appreciate her husband's triumph. Worship, perhaps more than any other Christian practice, reveals the heart, and Michal's response reveals to us that she has lost any faith in God that she may have once possessed.

We can understand Michal's loss. Years of frustration and delays obviously took their toll on her belief in God and His promises. But David suffered during that time as well, yet maintained his belief in God. Where did Michal go wrong?

Of course we don't know for sure, but I suspect Michal's downfall might have been allowing her faith to shift from being centered on who God is to what was happening around her. Remember, our faith is based solely on the *person* of God—His goodness, kindness, power, and absolute commitment to accomplish His will in our lives. God Himself is the guarantee that what He promises will be achieved. Our faith will suffer when we take our eyes off God and begin to focus on the circumstances around us that may not appear to be coming in line with God's promises. When God showed the Old Testament prophet Ezekiel a valley of decaying bones and asked him if the bones could once again live, he was asking Ezekiel to believe in His power to command life as the God of all existence, not asking Ezekiel to put his faith in the ability of dry bones to suddenly rejuvenate themselves.[14] Too often, we take our eyes off God and begin to focus on our circumstances, and our faith weakens as a result.

Consider David's experiences with the promises of God. He endured many of the same circumstances that Michal did: delay, hardship, loneliness, and much frustration in the wilderness. Certainly at times he must have questioned whether God's promise to make him king of Israel would ever come to pass. But if we examine the prayers he wrote to God during his time in the wilderness, we see that David resolutely keeps his eyes on God and not on his circumstances. Psalms 34, 52, 54, 56, 57, 59, and 142 were written during David's exile, and they each reveal David's steadfast focus on God alone. In Psalm 52, after Saul orders Doeg the Edomite to kill eighty-five priests and their families for helping David, David writes, "I trust in God's unfailing love for ever and ever."[15] When the Philistines break their alliance with David without cause, David keeps his focus simple in Psalm 56: "This I know: God is on my side!"[16] In Psalm 54, after Saul is closing in on David after receiving details of where David is hiding from the Ziphites, David writes, "You have delivered me from all my troubles, and my eyes have looked in triumph on my foes."[17] Such faith! Always, David's focus is on who the Lord is and not on what he sees happening around him.

THE REWARDS OF FAITH

When God does fulfill what he has promised, it is not Michal but David who enjoys the fruits of true faith: reward, intimacy, and freedom. David has received his reward for faithful belief in God's promises—rule over a united Israel. And he receives even more than that. After the ark returns to Jerusalem, 2 Samuel 7:16 records a new promise of God given to David by the prophet Nathan: "Your house and your kingdom will endure forever before me; your throne will be established forever." David's prayer immediately following Nathan's prophecy reveals the king's intimacy with the Lord; at one point in the prayer, David is rendered speechless as he ponders his love for God and the Lord's goodness to him.[18] Lastly, David is free. Free from obsessing over what could have been, free from bitterness over his years as a fugitive, free to worship God and trust Him to continue to lead and bless him. David has suffered the same disappointments and twists of fate that Michal has endured, but his trust in God remains strong, and he becomes known throughout the ages as a man who committed his way to God with passionate faith.

Michal, unfortunately, reaps a different legacy. In fact, our fairy-tale princess ends up living *un*happily ever after. After David's rebuke of Michal for despising his enthusiastic celebration before the Lord, the record in 2 Samuel 6 ends in the next verse with these chilling words: "And Michal daughter of Saul had no children to the day of her death."[19] Michal does not enjoy the fruits of faith as David does, and she does not receive the fulfillment of God's promises. She is left barren and alone, cut off from the lineage of David, plagued by her own anger and bitterness. Instead of becoming a Scriptural model of unwavering faith for future followers of God, Michal is a warning to believers of how difficult the passionate Christian life can become when we fail to develop and maintain the spiritual attribute of faith.

So where are you on your journey of faith? Perhaps you are still unsure of your relationship with God, struggling to commit yourself entirely to Him. Maybe you are working to believe the promises in Scripture, all of which are yes and amen in our Lord Jesus,[20] or perhaps you are growing in trusting God for a specific promise He has given you. Maybe you are like Michal, suffering a current loss of faith and questioning God. Regardless of the specifics, consider which step you need to take next—listening to the Holy Spirit to create a firm foundation for your faith, making the choice to act decisively, remembering and declaring God's truth and turning over the details to Him, or refocusing your faith on God Himself rather than on your circumstances. As you apply these suggestions, your faith in God will mature and strengthen and your passion for God will increase. Place these verses where you can see them every day and thank God for His unending, unfailing love and care for us:

> Surely the righteous will never be shaken;
>   they will be remembered forever.
> They will have no fear of bad news;
>   their hearts are steadfast, trusting in the Lord.
> Their hearts are secure, they will have no fear;
>   in the end they will look in triumph on their foes.
> They have freely scattered their gifts to the poor,
>   their righteousness endures forever;
>   their horn will be lifted high in honor.

(Psalm 112:6–9)

04: VISION

RESISTING STAGNATION

Name the greatest achievement of human vision you can think of—the Taj Mahal, the Empire State Building, the Roman Colosseum, the Great Wall of China, the Death Star? Impressive, yes, but I've got one better. How about an M&M? Smaller in size than a dime, the M&M is one of the most popular and recognizable candies in the world and produces an annual revenue of more than one billion dollars for candy company Mars Incorporated.[1] One M&M takes a day to make, the unique coating method that creates its hard candy shell occupying half the time.[2] And it comes in more than twenty colors. Now that's an achievement!

The vision for the M&M came from Forrest Mars, Sr., son of the founder of Mars Incorporated, when he saw soldiers in the Spanish Civil War in the 1930s eating chocolates coated in candy shells. He patented his own process, eventually branding each candy with the now-iconic "M." Mars Incorporated is one of the largest private companies in America and is known for its commitment to its original vision, summed up in the "Five Principles of Mars": quality, responsibility, mutuality, efficiency, and freedom. *Fortune* magazine has placed Mars on its list of the 100 Best Companies to Work For, in large part because Mars employees "love not only the products they make but also the office culture and the company's longstanding principles."[3] Vision like that of Mars Incorporated creates an environment in which both achievement and enjoyment are possible.

Vision is the ability to imagine both a future and the path to achieve it. Seeing the potential in a person, situation, institution, or philosophy provides a goal and a purpose. Setting a path toward that goal brings the vision into reality. These two pieces, imagining a creative future and motivating yourself and others to move toward it, are the keys to a successful vision.

Think back to a recent achievement you enjoyed—perhaps a recovered relationship, a professional success, or a physical accomplishment. How long was that goal in your mind and dreams before you realized it? Chances are that it was part of your thinking and planning for weeks, months, maybe even years. Envisioning your accomplishment and working steadily toward it enabled you to achieve success.

God is the ultimate visionary. Before the creation of the world, He imagined a reality in which His love would be poured into relationship with a people who

would bear His mark and reciprocate His faithfulness and affection. Even before the incident in Eden with the serpent, God envisioned the sacrifice Jesus
would make for human sin, as well as a people to be His own "before the creation of the world."[4] God's very first words after Adam and Eve plunged man-
kind into sin in the Garden of Eden included the promise of Jesus, the One who
would "crush" the power of Satan and redeem humans from the Fall.[5] The Old
and New Testaments are full of God's prophetic promises concerning His plan
for humanity and His kingdom. God is remarkably forward-thinking and intentional for the good of the world and for the individual believer as well.

He created each of us to be unique, and His vision for each of us is also
unique. To accomplish this vision, God will weave together the professional,
physical, emotional, and relational aspects of our lives in distinctive ways to accomplish His purposes. As we follow God, our lives reflect purpose and direction, and we experience the blossoming into who we are meant to be.

Hudson Taylor, born in 1832, was an English missionary to China, serving that country for fifty-one years. He was known as a man who had a vision
from God for what he could accomplish in his lifetime, and he pursued that
vision with all his heart. Taylor broke many rules of nineteenth-century mis-
siology during his time in China—dressing in Chinese clothing and respect-
ing Chinese culture; avoiding denominational affiliation; accepting unmarried
women and members of the working class as missionaries; and campaigning
against England's opium trade in China, a trade that devastated Chinese health
and economy, but was stunningly lucrative for England. Taylor even founded
his own mission agency, China Inland Mission, so he could pursue God's purposes single-mindedly. In an account Taylor wrote of his vision for China titled
China's Spiritual Need and Claim, Taylor opens the book with these words: "It is
a solemn and most momentous truth that our every act in this present life—and
our every omission too—has a direct and important bearing both on our own
future welfare, and on that of others."[6] Hudson Taylor understood that God has
a vision for each of our lives.

Sadly, we modern Christians are often rather unlike Hudson Taylor and his
pursuit of God's vision, instead being regrettably backward-thinking and un-
intentional when it comes to maintaining vision in our lives. I frequently ask
Christians I meet to share with me God's vision for their lives and am continually surprised when they usually have no answer. Most of them have never even
considered that God has a specific calling for them. I believe that this absence
of intentionality contributes to the lack of spiritual passion in our lives. Without
vision, excitement for following Jesus can wane as we have no clear goals to
pursue. Bereft of motivating goals, we may experience stagnation. Like a cess-
pool that has no outlet to offer nourishment to others and no inlet to receive

new, healthy water for itself, a life without vision will become torpid and dull, evidencing little of God's power and passion. We can feel stuck—struggling with the same sins, straining against the same doubts, and passively accepting the same meager spiritual fruit in our lives because we have no vision for anything better. No wonder the Bible cautions believers that "where there is no vision, the people perish."[7] Or, as the old adage warns, if you aim at nothing, you'll hit it.

I suspect that much of our failure to seize God's vision for us springs from not understanding the process God uses to convey and accomplish His plans in our lives. Quite simply, God's vision is imparted to us in three stages: the *call*, the *preparation*, and the *fulfillment*. By examining how God works out this process in one biblical woman's life, we can see the steps more clearly and concretely for ourselves.

Miriam, sister of both the Old Testament prophet Moses and high priest Aaron, is born when the Israelites are slaves in ancient Egypt. As a young girl, Miriam saves her brother Moses from certain death when the Egyptian ruler Pharaoh orders that all Israelite baby boys be killed. She suffers for decades as a slave while Moses is in exile, joining him as a leader of her people when he is sent back to Egypt by God to deliver the Israelites from their bondage. After the people of God escape from the Egyptians by walking through the Red Sea on dry land, Miriam leads the nation in a song of praise to the Lord. Her later descent into jealousy and pride while journeying to the Promised Land also is recorded in Scripture, when Miriam joins with Aaron to question Moses' leadership of the people. She is punished by God with leprosy, but ultimately receives His forgiveness and restoration and is honored in Micah 6:4 as a leader provided by God for His people. Let's look at how Miriam pursues God's vision for her through her call, preparation, and fulfillment.

THE CALL

All my life, I've been told I have a very distinctive speaking voice. Once people hear me talk, they often offer suggestions about how I could parlay my unique voice into a successful career. I am sorry to say that the careers suggested are never vocally flattering ones such as opera singer, meditation instructor, or horse whisperer. No, the recommendations usually fall more along the lines of radio announcer, basketball coach, or drill sergeant. Apparently, my voice cuts through ambient noise rather well (and, as a college professor who typically teaches early morning classes, I have found it quite beneficial for keeping students awake).

Although I've always attempted to receive these suggestions graciously, I have never felt that following one of them was my calling. Perhaps you also have experienced others telling you what your call should be, what you should be doing with your life, or where you should be headed. Or maybe you have experienced the opposite—the unsettling feeling that you have no idea whatsoever why you were put on this earth. Either way, if we want to embrace God's vision for us, we have to start by seeking His call on our lives.

But what do I mean by God's "call"? Quite simply, God's call on our lives is the potent combination of who we are and what we will do with our lives. Our calling is the foundation for God's vision for us and our future. Who we are is a one-of-a-kind mixture of our spiritual gifting, personality, resources, desires, dreams, and more. What we will do is composed of the distinctive plans God has for our life. As God promises us in Jeremiah 29:11, His plans for us are to bless us, endowing us with "hope and a future." And God's calling is not based on our merit, but is for His glory. In 1 Corinthians 1:28–29, we are reminded that "God chose the lowly things of this world and the despised things—and the things that are not—to nullify the things that are, so that no one may boast before him." God intends to use each one of us in effective and powerful ways in His kingdom through ministry, relationships, occupation, avocations, and more. This unique combination of who we are and what we do makes up our call. The details will look different at different times in our lives, but the essence of God's call on our lives will be consistent.

Hudson Taylor's call was to be a man who shared God's offer of salvation to those outside his culture. The specific activities of his call included preaching, offering medical services, and establishing a mission agency. Similarly, I have learned that my personal call from God is to be a woman who seeks and worships God, teaches others, and helps Christians move into the destinies God has for them. This is who I am. The activities that make up that call for me have included teaching Bible classes at my church, working as a professor in a university, leading prayer groups, writing small group Bible study materials, and mentoring college students and young Christians. These activities are what I do.

Let's look at Miriam's call. In Exodus 15:19–21, it is written: "When Pharaoh's horses, chariots and horsemen went into the sea, the Lord brought the waters of the sea back over them, but the Israelites walked through the sea on dry ground. Then Miriam the prophet, Aaron's sister, took a timbrel in her hand, and all the women followed her, with timbrels and dancing. Miriam sang to them: 'Sing to the Lord, / for he is highly exalted. / Both horse and driver / he has hurled into the sea.'" Similarly, Micah 6:4 notes, "I brought you [Israelites] up out of Egypt and redeemed you from the land of slavery. I sent Moses to lead you, also Aaron and Miriam." So Miriam is both a prophet and leader of Israel. That is her call. The activities that flow from this call for Miriam include defying Pharaoh's orders to save her brother's life as well as leading God's people in a song of worship after their deliverance at the Red Sea. These activities will vary according to the different seasons of Miriam's life, but they will always reflect God's call for her.

So how do we find God's calling for us—that powerful combination of who we are and what we are created to do? Miriam's early life gives us some hints. Miriam first enters the scriptural narrative as a young girl, a Hebrew slave living in Egypt. The Israelites have been enslaved by the Egyptians for four hundred years, and the current Pharaoh has decreed that all Israelite infant boys must be killed to curtail the rapid growth of the Hebrew population. When Miriam's mother delivers Moses, she recognizes that he is special to God and hides him for three months. When she can no longer hide him, she places him in a basket and settles him among the reeds on the bank of the Nile River. Miriam stands watch over the basket and, when Moses is pulled from the water by Pharaoh's daughter, she runs to the princess and offers to find a Hebrew woman to nurse the baby. Pharaoh's daughter agrees, and so Miriam brings her mother to nurture Moses until he is older and is adopted by Pharaoh's daughter.[8]

Miriam's early life shows us several important steps for finding our call from God. First, do not allow your call to be defined by any current obstacles or challenges in your life. Miriam was a slave, an institution that is intentionally designed to produce the exact opposite of vision, particularly the race-based, hereditary slavery that Miriam and the people of Israel endured in ancient Egypt. As a slave, Miriam certainly experienced the fear, powerlessness, hopelessness, and insecurity that accompany unpaid servitude for life, yet she reveals a remarkable sense of self-confidence in asking the daughter of Pharaoh to break her own father's law and keep a Hebrew baby. We cannot allow our current challenges to dictate God's call for us because God is bigger than our obstacles.

Second, listen to the Holy Spirit and people you respect when evaluating who God has made you to be and what you are called to do. The book of Proverbs is so full of instruction about seeking wise counselors for your life (Proverbs 12:15, 11:14, 19:20, 24:6, 27:9, etc.) that it is almost the Eleventh Commandment. Miriam's mother obviously recognized that Miriam was a person who could protect Moses and problem-solve when the need arose, and the young Miriam did a stellar job of both. Who has spoken into your life regarding your gifts, abilities, and purpose from God? Your parents, spouse, children, friends, pastor, employer, neighbor, Bible study leader? Ask them what they see in you that is unique and can be used in God's kingdom.

I have a friend who leads the small group ministry at a nondenominational megachurch. Years ago, when she was just a college student, her InterVarsity Christian Fellowship campus advisors noticed her leadership qualities and ability to bring people together effectively in small group settings. By recognizing her early spiritual passion for community and sharing with her what they saw as God's vision for her life, those campus fellowship advisors launched my friend onto a path of small group ministry that has continued throughout the different stages of her life: leading college and graduate school groups as a student, coordinating new mothers' groups with the local chapter of Mothers of Preschoolers as a stay-at-home mom, and currently overseeing diverse adult groups as well as serving on the board of a national organization for small group ministry. The core of my friend's calling to help foster biblical community has not changed over the decades, even as the expression of her calling has adapted to varying environments and life stages. In a similar way, those wise Christians around you can help you understand and identify significant parts of God's call for you.

Third, pay attention to your own personal experiences with the Lord and how He has worked in your life in the past, to understand the specifics of your unique calling. Miriam transitioned from being her infant brother's caretaker to caring for and leading the people of Israel. Think about yourself and your own experiences. Are you the person to whom everyone comes when they are struggling? Perhaps God has given you the spiritual gift of counseling. Are you the one who is always asked to plan and lead the church retreat? Maybe leadership or administrative efficiency is part of your makeup. Are you the individual who encourages others and makes everyone feel welcome in your home? Maybe hospitality is part of your calling. Know yourself and take notice of how the Lord uses you. Ask the Holy Spirit to reveal to you the uniqueness of how He has made you. Invite godly leaders to identify where they've seen you serving effectively in the church. These answers will lead you to knowing who you are and what you are called to do.

Lastly, once you have a sense of God's call for you, commit to it and reinforce it in your life. Specifically, adjust your sense of self so that it matches God's vision for you. Agree with God about who He has made you to be and see yourself as God sees you. Sounds simple? It is simple. What it is not, however, is easy. Your calling as a unique follower of God is assaulted at every turn. Popular culture, words spoken over you as a child, insults hurled at you by those close to you, lies suggested by Satan himself—all these hindrances conspire to make you believe you are who they say you are. But you are not. You are who God says you are. And the more you reinforce that identity and calling, the more God's truth will become a foundation for vision.

We reinforce God's call for us by adjusting our thoughts, words, and actions to come into line with our calling. The thoughts we allow into our heads, the words we speak, and the behavioral choices we make should consistently support what we know about who God has made us to be and what we are called to do. If God has shown you that you are an encourager who makes others feel valued, do not publicly criticize the head of your church's youth ministry who irritated you last week. That is not in line with your calling. If you are called as an intercessor to pray for others, refuse to engage with the voice in your head that says you never hear God right. That is not in line with your calling. If you are given new responsibilities in your job because you are a leader, politely ignore the naysayer who tells you that you are not equipped for the role. That is not in line with your calling. Use every ounce of energy to think, speak, and act in line with the calling you have received from God.

If such personal vigilance sounds overwhelming and exhausting, remember that as believers we have the Holy Spirit in our lives, and so everything we do and experience is done in the context of relationship with God. He is always there to encourage us, to direct us, and to love us, so we can trust His power that works within us to conform us to the image of Jesus. The God of love who has given us life and our calling will keep us and help us grow in all of these areas. So we take one or two simple steps, pressing forward, rejoicing in the strength God gives us to continue growing.

THE PREPARATION

I always love to read the story in Genesis in which Joseph receives a dream from the Lord that he will be a ruler, and then he is invited to become the youngest leader in all of Egypt. Or the story of when Abraham is told that he will finally have a son, and then Sarah delivers a baby nine months later. Or especially the tale in which Jewish religious leader Saul stops persecuting Christians and becomes a follower of Jesus, jumping on the next ship for the Gentile world to preach and lead others to the Savior. What? Those stories don't happen that way? Are you sure? Because I'm pretty certain that once you get a call from God, things fall into place pretty quickly and easily. Are you saying it doesn't always work that way?

Well, of course I am being facetious, because if there is one truth about living out God's vision for us, it is that when we hear a call from God, we usually are not quite ready to answer. Joseph had to learn humility before he began to rule, Abraham failed to wait on his heavenly father before he became the father of nations, and Saul had to become Paul and spend three years in the deserts of Arabia before being called as a missionary.[9] As believers, we often make two mistakes when we become aware of God's calling on our lives. First, we expect that we will see the fulfillment of God's vision for us unfold immediately, or at least pretty quickly. That is seldom the case. The reason that we rarely see immediate fulfillment is that God is not interested in calling us to something that we already can do. No, He desires to call us to something *more* than what we can even imagine for ourselves—something that will stretch us, challenge us, and be totally incredible. He wants to grow us into the person that fits the amazing call He has for us. And that takes time.

Second, we can make the mistake of undervaluing the preparation process. Sometimes the preparation time looks like a desert—Joseph languished in prison, Abraham panicked and fathered Ishmael who would not be the son of the promise, and Paul suffered the rejection of many Christians who did not believe he had really become a follower of Christ. Without a doubt, all of these men struggled with feeling like their lives were being wasted while they labored during their times of preparation. But it is exactly this time of living in the desert that produces the greatest growth in our lives and makes us the people of God's vision.

Hudson Taylor committed to going to China as a missionary in 1849, but he did not arrive there until 1854. Was that time wasted as Taylor waited for God's vision to be realized in his life? Certainly not. During those years, Taylor took advantage of his time of preparation, studying Mandarin, pursuing training in medicine, dispensing gospel tracts, and practicing open-air preaching. When he finally arrived in China, he was the man God needed him to be to pioneer a new way of ministry to the Chinese.

Miriam also experiences a time of preparation, as God prepares her to be the woman of His vision. After saving her infant brother Moses, Miriam endures a life of slavery while Moses spends his days in the royal palace. After Moses kills an Egyptian overseer for beating a Hebrew slave, he escapes hundreds of miles away to Midian and spends the next forty years working as a shepherd. We are not told about Miriam's life during Moses' youth and subsequent exile, but we are told in Exodus that the Egyptian overlords made life extremely difficult for the Hebrew slaves, so Miriam's many decades of preparation were probably painful and frustrating.

Of all the seasons I've experienced so far in life, my years as a stay-at-home mom were probably my least impressive. I was never one of those mothers who naturally seemed to know what to do in parenting situations—like how to politely manage the playground bully, when to step in and stop the sibling rivalry, or what to say when the unimaginable horror of being the first to get out in the spelling bee became a reality. But I did make one good decision during my decade at home with kids: I used my time off from work and other out-of-the-home responsibilities to spend quality time with the Lord and deepen my intimacy with him. It certainly didn't feel like I was accomplishing much during that time, dawdling away my morning hours and kids' naptimes by praying and learning to wait on God, but soon after my youngest child went off to kindergarten, the Lord began opening up opportunities for me to speak and teach in the church. Interestingly, the speaking topic most often requested of me was how to develop intimacy with God. Thankfully, I had a whole notebook of experiences and practical suggestions to share with others as the importance of my preparation time became increasingly obvious to me. Had I resigned myself to simply enduring those years as only boring or useless, I would not have been ready to step into the new things God had for me when my time of preparation was completed.

When you are in a time of preparation, *press in.* Learn the lessons God is teaching you. Pursue His presence and voice. Change the unhelpful habits and wrong thinking that are holding you back. Read books, study Scripture, attend sound teaching, and spend time with believers who can help you grow. Basically, see your desert experience—whether it is forty days or forty years—as the most important time of your life. This is the key time to hold on, learn and grow, and trust God and His process. Preparation time is never wasted. You will see the fruit of your preparation when the time of fulfillment comes.

FULFILLMENT

Fulfillment is the time when the vision we have preserved and pursued finally comes to fruition. As Christians, fulfillment is when we step into all that God has promised us. It is the fulfillment of God's call, and we are ready to embrace it because of our growth during our time of preparation.

If we have been diligent in our training, we will know when God's hand is ready to move. Miriam experiences this moment when Moses returns from Midian and reveals to the Hebrew elders and the people that God has decided to deliver them from their bondage. The people believe Moses and worship God for His concern for them.[10] This is the moment they have been waiting for—God is going to release them from their oppression.

But recognizing the moment of fulfillment is not enough by itself. We must also step forward in faith. Miriam and the people of Israel now have to move forward into their new life, trusting God as they live through the ten plagues, the increased workload and compounded anger of Pharaoh, and the dangerous exit out of Egypt. But move forward they do, and simple footsteps become historic miracles as they end up walking through the Red Sea on dry land.

Stepping forward into God's calling for you may require adopting a new thought pattern. It may mean a change in habits. It may mean a move across the country, a job change, a financial commitment, another child, a sacrifice of time, a new ministry, a change in scheduling, or more. We know from our own past experiences that stepping into something new requires us to relinquish something old. Our hands must be empty to receive the fresh offering God has for us.

However, stepping into something new can sometimes feel less like fulfillment and more like leaping off a cliff. We may want to hold on to the past because it is what we know; it is safe, secure, and comforting. Countless examples exist of people remaining in difficult, stressful, stagnant, or even abusive situations because they are afraid of the unknown. Even the Israelites hesitated at the banks of the Red Sea, unsure whether they should move forward and trust God. The predictability of Egypt appeared very attractive to them at that moment. Singer/songwriter Sarah Groves identifies the Israelites' desire to return to the security of Egyptian enslavement as a natural human tendency in her song "Painting Pictures of Egypt":

> The past is so tangible
> I know it by heart
> Familiar things are never easy to discard
> I was dying for some freedom but now I hesitate to go
> I am caught between the promise and the things I know.

Moving forward into God's vision for us can be scary.

But, in our heart of hearts, we know that to see fulfillment of God's vision for us, we honestly don't have a choice but to move forward. Once God decides to bring something new, staying in the same place is really the same as moving backward. Groves recognizes this reality in her song as well:

> I've been painting pictures of Egypt
> Leaving out what it lacks
> The future feels so hard and I want to go back
> But the places that used to fit me cannot hold the things I've learned
> And those roads were closed off to me while my back was turned.[11]

I love that image—the road back is closed off while we are learning and growing into the new person God is making us to be. The old reality just doesn't "fit" us anymore. In the Israelites' case, the road back is literally closed off by a giant wall of water called the Red Sea, which closes back in on itself and the Egyptian soldiers who are pursuing the fleeing Israelites. In a dramatic manner, the Israelites are free and on their way to the fulfillment of God's promise to them of a land of their own.

Fulfillment of God's calling on her life has come for Miriam personally as well. After walking between walls of water into her destiny, Miriam leads the women in praise to God and delivers a prophetic word to the people. She is recognized as a prophet, and so her word is received and appreciated by the people. She is accepted as a leader, and so her instructions to dance before the Lord in worship are followed. Miriam has stepped into the fulfillment of God's vision for her, birthed so many years earlier on the banks of the Nile River.

PUTTING IT ALL TOGETHER

This process of hearing God's call, embracing the time of preparation, and stepping into fulfillment is cyclical and will be repeated throughout our lifetime as the Lord works in different areas of our lives. Living out your calling is not a once-and-done thing. It is a lifelong process. Trust that God will finish the work He has begun in you. Your responsibility in this is to try to recognize the stage of the process that you are in. Can you feel God stirring something in you? Perhaps you should seek His potential call in that area. Are you experiencing a time of tension and stretching? Don't immediately blame Satan or try to escape from it; maybe God is looking for you to grow in an area in which He intends for you to blossom. Are you on the brink of something new? It's possible that God is ready to bring you into deeper fulfillment of His vision for you; don't be afraid to take the next step.

And, above all, do not let failure stop you. After many experiences in the desert and only a few months from the Promised Land, Miriam experiences a failure that would make even the stoutest heart despair. Envious of Moses' greater prophetic gifting, she and Aaron condemn Moses before the people, and God punishes Miriam by giving her leprosy. She is sent outside the camp for seven days. But forgiveness and restoration come to Miriam, as she is eventually healed by Moses' intercession for her. The people of Israel do not break camp until Miriam rejoins them, a sign that God still recognizes her as a leader in Israel, despite her failing.[12] We will each experience failure in differing degrees as we seek to hear God's call, respond during times of preparation, and fulfill our callings. As Miriam's example shows us, God is always ready to forgive and reestablish us when we repent and turn to Him. Don't let failure stop you from moving into the vision that God has for you!

05: INITIATIVE

THWARTING PASSIVITY

Our study thus far has focused on the internal attributes conducive to developing a passionate spiritual life: devotion that conquers discontentment, courage that faces fear, faith that defeats doubt, and vision that resists stagnation. These attributes spring up from inside of us, flowing from the Living Water we receive from God. But merely an internal commitment to a passionate spiritual life is not enough. As believers, we must also develop godly characteristics to interact with the society in which we live. In the parable of the soils, Jesus identifies the forces arrayed against believers—the kingdom of darkness that snatches up God's truth before it can properly implant, the trouble and persecution that reveal a lack of rootedness in authentic belief, and the cares and wealth of the world that choke the fruitfulness out of spirituality.[1] As those called to share God's healing from the river of the water of life with a hurting world, we must be willing to be pioneers who take the initiative and thwart passivity, to be nonconformists who battle indifference, to be tenacious conquerors who break through rejection, and to be generous life-givers who help overcome despair. Let's begin our look at these four external attributes of a spiritual life of passion and power by examining *initiative*.

THE REAL ONE

In *The Sun Also Rises*, Ernest Hemingway's quintessential novel of the post-World War I "Lost Generation," the main characters (all ex-veterans of the Great War) spend their time gallivanting around Europe, drinking, smoking, fighting, and racking up casual sexual encounters. The characters are noteworthy particularly for their impotence—for the narrator Jake, physically, and for the other characters, practically. One is a bankrupt British socialite, another a boxing champion turned novelist with two failed relationships, another a hopeless gambler, and another a restless *femme fatale* bent on using meaningless hookups to forget her one true love who was lost in the war. The one defining characteristic of all of them is an inability to initiate anything worthwhile. They drift aimlessly through Paris and Pamplona, being knocked about by their carnal desires, the people they meet, and a society into which they no longer fit. They are exactly the type of people Paul promises his readers they can avoid becoming if they seek true maturity in Christ in Ephesians 4:14: "Then we will no longer be infants, tossed back and forth by the waves, and blown here and there by every wind of teaching and by the cunning and craftiness of people in their deceitful scheming."

In Pamplona for the bullfights, our hapless gang bumps into the absolute opposite of themselves—a man who knows who he is, what he wants, and is willing to commit himself to getting it. Pedro Romero, a young, talented bull-fighting prodigy of nineteen is the "real one," the one who has true bullfighting *aficion*, or passion. Romero stands out in the novel as the only character to show true initiative in pursuing his dreams, and although our crew of expatriates tries to lure him into their ill-fated circle, he resists. By the end of the novel, Romero has rejected the sexually destructive woman no other man can resist, outlasted the reckless boxing champion who knocked out every other man with a single punch, and established himself as the greatest bullfighter of the fiesta. No one else can measure up.

When we encounter a person like Romero, we are drawn to their willingness to take charge of a situation and make things happen. Initiative is the ability to not simply respond to situations but to instigate, activate, and prompt authentically proactive exploits. A life characterized by spiritual passion requires initiative because without it our passivity will place us at the mercy of a world that does not know or love Christ and certainly does not want to help us in our attempts to bring His blessing and healing to others. The Old Testament book of Proverbs is an entire manuscript devoted to teaching believers how to pursue change in their lives instead of passively responding to the world. Its opening lines include the admonition in verse 1:8 to pursue godliness: "Listen, my son, to your father's instruction and do not forsake your mother's teaching." Particularly when we can be used by God to bless others, we are encouraged to "not withhold good from those who deserve it, when it is in your power to act. Do not say to your neighbor, 'Come back later; I'll give it tomorrow.'"[2] God is looking for passionate followers who are willing to take the initiative and change the world, not just react to it, or, worse yet, be changed by it.

Another person who survived a war, but with more success than Hemingway's troop, is a woman mentioned in 2 Samuel 20, and she will help us understand the role of initiative in a passionate spiritual life. At the time of this story, David is king of all twelve of the tribes of Israel and has already survived a rebellion and attempted *coup* by his son Absalom, when another insurrection arises. Perhaps angered at the transfer of power to David's tribe of Judah from Saul's tribe of Benjamin, a man from the tribe of Benjamin named Sheba rebels against David's rule and attempts to draw men to his cause. He travels throughout the country, gathering soldiers to fight on his side, eventually landing with his band of rebels in a town far north of Jerusalem named Abel Beth Maakah.

King David sends his military commander Joab with an army to besiege the city, and they build a siege ramp and begin battering the walls. Disaster for the people of Abel Beth Maakah seems imminent, but the city is saved by a quick thinking, unnamed woman who takes the initiative and resolves the situation before the city's walls are overrun and the town destroyed.[3] The story of her resourcefulness is the focus of this chapter.

PIONEER MINDSET

A few years ago, the History Channel ran a miniseries called *The Bible*. One of my favorite scenes was when Mary the mother of Jesus tells Joseph that she is pregnant with the Messiah. The writers of the series read between the lines of Scripture and imagined what that conversation might have sounded like as Mary implores, "Please, Joseph. I need you to be my husband. I need you to be the father of this child. The child of God. Please, my love. Please trust me." Joseph's response to her plea is stunning in its humanness: "Mary, God doesn't do this to people like us."[4]

Have you ever felt like God was asking you to do something beyond your capabilities? Perhaps not quite as challenging as parenting the Son of God, but something that you felt you could not handle? Often, taking initiative requires us to step into something new, undertake a challenge we might find daunting, or envision unique ways to solve a problem. We must go where no one has gone before, we must face unknown challenges, and we must develop original paths forward. In reality, taking initiative will often mean that we must be pioneers. That's why taking initiative for God's kingdom will often require what I call a pioneer mindset—an outlook that is not afraid to step forward and blaze a new trail. A pioneer mindset helps us initiate in two ways: we maintain God's perspective on the situation, and we recognize the importance of the role we are called to play.

God's perspective on any situation is always hopeful and forward-looking. As the God of the universe, He does not experience fear, hesitation, or uncertainty; everything He plans will be accomplished, and it will be good. As Job recognizes during his encounter with God in the Old Testament: "I know that you can do all things; no purpose of yours can be thwarted."[5] So when God asks us to take the initiative, he knows it will ultimately be a blessing in our lives and in the lives of others. As humans, of course, we are prone to focus on the difficulties, dangers, and challenges of a new or frightening situation. That is why maintaining God's perspective is so crucial to taking the initiative—it motivates us to keep moving forward.

When my husband received a job offer on the West Coast while we were living on the East Coast, I felt a bit like God was asking me to be a pioneer.

Both of our families had always lived in the mid-Atlantic region, and relocating our nuclear family to California was like uprooting an oak tree. Everything that makes up a life—friendships, family ties, church, neighborhood, schools—was not in the Golden State. But two weeks after the formal job offer and two days before school started, we moved across the country. Certainly an abrupt move across the nation offered numerous obstacles to command my attention, but a better choice was to remember the promises of God that I could count on. I knew that God promises to always be with me, that He promises to work things for good in my life, and that He promises to give me a hope and a future. By God's grace, these promises became my perspective as I dealt with our transcontinental transition (and, well, the consistently beautiful weather in southern California might have helped a bit as well).

In our story in 2 Samuel 20, Joab's army is about to knock down the walls of Abel Beth Maakah to reach the rebel Sheba and his men. Unless someone from inside the walls takes the initiative, the city is doomed. Suddenly, a woman from the city pokes her head over the wall and asks to speak to Joab. When Joab comes within earshot, the woman delivers this message: "Long ago they used to say, 'Get your answer at Abel,' and that settled it. We are the peaceful and faithful in Israel. You are trying to destroy a city that is a mother in Israel. Why do you want to swallow up the Lord's inheritance?"[6] Joab is taken aback by her challenge, and responds that they are simply seeking the rebel Sheba. He promises to withdraw if she will hand over Sheba. The woman agrees, and pledges that his head will be thrown over the city wall. The woman then gathers the people of the city, and they agree to her plan and cut off Sheba's head, sending it over the wall into Joab's grateful clutches. Joab withdraws and the city is saved.

Now this is a woman who is not afraid to take initiative! And her willingness to step forward and save her city flows in part from her ability to maintain God's perspective on the situation by focusing on God's truth and promises instead of the obstacles before her. In reality, the obstacles are many. She is a woman, with less legal and social standing than a man. She is not (as far as we can tell from the narrative) a military person, nor is she identified as a town elder or leader. She is also in the middle of an extremely tense wartime situation, fraught with danger for the entire town. What if Joab does not appreciate her rebuke? What if the people do not agree to help her follow through on the promise she makes to Joab?

Despite the risks, our heroine has one thing going for her—the Bible notes that she is "wise."[7] Wise people know that God's perspective is the only one that matters, and so this woman focuses on God's promises, both for herself and for Joab. She reminds Joab of God's purpose for Abel Beth Maakah: it is a city that reveals God's wisdom to His people, functioning as a mother to all Israel. It is a place of insight and understanding where God's children can hear the heart of God, and a center of peace and faithfulness in a time when rebellion and unrest are simmering among the tribes of Israel. It is part of God's inheritance for the people of Israel, a gift from Him that should be treasured, not destroyed. Reminding herself and Joab of God's perspective on the situation enables our heroine to take steps that save the city.

But this woman also knows that the second part of a pioneer mindset is embracing the role God has called us to play, even if the role surprises us. Did it make sense to her natural mind that she, a simple woman of Abel Beth Maakah, would be the one God was calling to end the military siege against her city by the armies of King David? I doubt it. Certainly there were greater military minds than hers attacking the problem. But she was the one chosen by God to end the standoff without innocent bloodshed, and she is immortalized in Scripture for her willingness to play the role God assigned her. If she had not stepped forward with her plan, many lives could have been lost as a result.

The astounding truth about life as a Christian is that God has a role for each of us to play in His kingdom that can only be fulfilled by us in our time on earth. As we know from Paul's explanation of the body of Christ in 1 Corinthians 12, a foot cannot become a hand and an ear cannot become an eye; the body needs all parts to survive and thrive.[8] Just so, we who make up the body of believers must each recognize our indispensability to that body and initiate the actions God has called us to perform, just as our heroine did.

What has God asked you to do? Are you waiting for someone else to step in and handle it? Will there be someone more qualified than you to parent your children, encourage your spouse, finish the project at work, minister to the elderly couple down the street, or reach out to the needy in your neighborhood? Not if God has called you to the job. The sobering reality is that no one else in the body of Christ can make up for us not playing our role—no matter how supremely gifted, resourced, or trained our intended replacement may be. God wants us each to recognize how crucial we are to His plans, and this attitude adjustment is part of developing the pioneer mindset necessary to initiate action in God's kingdom.

PIONEERS TAKE RISKS

A pioneering mindset that focuses on God's perspective and promises instead of obstacles and that recognizes the importance of our role in God's plan will lead directly to pioneer actions, and we can identify four pioneering actions in our heroine's story. The first pioneer action of this woman of Abel Beth Maakah is that she is willing to take a risk. She is prepared to endanger her reputation, her standing in the community, and even her personal safety when she initiates her plan to save the city. Joab could have responded vindictively to her rebuke, the townspeople could have turned against her for promising something they did not intend to deliver, or Sheba's followers in the city could have attacked her for her suggestion to lop off his head. Sometimes, taking initiative means that we must assume some personal risk, either to relationships, finances, reputation, or even safety.

The founders of the United States of America were willing to assume great personal risk when they initiated independence from Great Britain (the mightiest nation in the world at the time) by signing the Declaration of Independence on July 4, 1776. Their willingness to risk life and property may have been encouraged by a pamphlet published six months earlier titled *Common Sense*, the first pamphlet published in the colonies to advocate an immediate declaration of independence from Great Britain, and a runaway bestseller. Written by an Englishman named Thomas Paine who had emigrated to Philadelphia, *Common Sense* revealed to the colonists the far-reaching effects of their current choices:

> The cause of America is in great measure the cause of all mankind.... 'Tis not the concern of a day, a year, or an age; posterity are virtually involved in the contest, and will be more or less affected even to the end of time, by the proceedings now. Now is the seed time of continental union, faith and honor. The least fracture now will be like a name engraved with the point of a pin on the tender rind of a young oak; the wound would enlarge with the tree, and posterity read it in full grown characters.[9]

Just as the smallest letters scratched into a young sapling will become enormous words when the tree reaches maturity, so our actions have ultimate consequences for ourselves and others that will far outweigh any personal risks. Paine's words galvanized the nation, and, half a year later, fifty-six men willingly signed a Declaration of Independence that ends with these words: "And for the support of this Declaration, with a firm reliance on the protection of Divine Providence, we mutually pledge to each other our Lives, our Fortunes, and our sacred Honor." A willingness to take risks is necessary to initiate the actions of a passionate life.

A second pioneering action taken by our heroine to save her city is that she decides on a concrete course of action that solves the problem—she offers to sacrifice the life of one rebellious man to save the entire city. Initiative requires that we decide on practical, tangible steps to accomplish our goal. The need to make realistic choices to achieve practical purposes is a well-known truth, but I have found that the same reality applies to spiritual goals as well. As Christians, we sometimes shy away from being practical when it comes to taking the initiative in our spiritual lives. Unfortunately, lofty, abstract spiritual goals will come to nothing without practical steps to achieve them. Do you want to grow in patience?

Don't just pray for patience; determine practical steps to achieve it. Maybe you will decide to memorize five Bible verses that relate to patience and place them throughout your house and car as reminders of your commitment to grow in that area. Hoping to grow in understanding God's word? Purchase a study Bible with explanatory notes, commit two hours every weekend to scripture study, and ask a teacher in your church to meet with you once a month to discuss principles of Bible study. Desiring to hear God's voice more clearly? Don't simply listen to a sermon on hearing God—choose to rest in silence in God's presence for ten minutes each day and keep a journal of words you hear from the Holy Spirit. Want to develop godly leadership skills? Ask if you can help colead one of the small groups for middle school students at your church during the summer, and take a public speaking class. Real spiritual growth is accomplished by initiating small, concrete steps toward your goal and sticking with them until they bear fruit. As God asks the prophet Zechariah, "Who despises the day of small things?"[10]

Our heroine demonstrates a third pioneering action when she leads others to get involved in her plan. According to 2 Samuel 20:22a, the woman "went to all the people with her wise advice, and they cut off the head of Sheba son of Bikri and threw it to Joab." Taking initiative often requires exhibiting authentic, godly leadership, and the woman of Abel Beth Maakah does just that when she rallies the people to support and implement her plan. It would be a safe bet to assume that she could not have fought her way through Sheba's men and killed him by herself. Her plan required the consensus and participation of the town, and I suspect she persuaded her neighbors to enact her plan in much the same way she convinced Joab of his folly in seeking to destroy the city: by pointing the people to God rather than to herself. The biblical narrative reveals that her "wise advice" convinced the people, not a forceful presence, status in the community, or military background and training. Godly leadership always points to the Lord rather than to ourselves and motivates people to believe in and work toward His purposes. This woman was able to lead the people of her city to catch God's vision for the solution to their problem, and they came behind her in support. Taking the initiative will often require the help of others; godly leadership that focuses on God and His purposes will point the way forward for everyone.

Lastly, our heroine finishes the job. Sheba's head is removed and tossed to Joab, and the siege is over. So often when we initiate new things in our lives, we end up stopping before the goal is fully achieved. Lack of self-discipline, misdirected focus, fatigue, loss of hope—so many obstacles can stop us from finishing what we started. The wise initiator will know that perseverance is required until the end, just as Jesus completed His assignment on earth and received the glory that was His due.

English politician William Wilberforce was a model of persevering until the job is done. Having become a Christian in his twenties, Wilberforce soon took on a project that he felt had been given to him by the Lord—the abolition of the slave trade in the British Empire. Taking black slaves from Africa across the ocean to be sold in the West Indies was making England an enormous profit in the late eighteenth century, and few in Britain believed anyone could bring a stop to the lucrative practice that was central to Britain's economic empire. However, Wilberforce believed with all his heart that he was called by God to fight on behalf of the voiceless and powerless:

> So enormous, so dreadful, so irremediable did the [slave] trade's wickedness appear that my own mind was completely made up for abolition. Let the consequences be what they would: I from this time determined that I would never rest until I had effected its abolition.

As early as 1789, Wilberforce began introducing resolutions against the slave trade into Parliament, but his bills were defeated in 1789, 1791, 1792, 1793, 1797, 1798, 1799, 1804, and 1805. It was not until 1807 that the slave trade in England was abolished and not until 1833 that the Slavery Abolition Act freed all slaves in the British Empire. Wilberforce died just three days after hearing that the passage of the Slavery Abolition Act was assured by Parliament.[11] Finishing strong is a key component in bringing what we initiate to a successful end.

SEEING RESULTS

The result of pursuing initiative in our lives is that instead of simply reacting to life and passively accepting what is doled out to us, we make a difference for ourselves and for others. We are used by God to bring lasting, powerful change into a world that deeply needs it. The woman of Abel Beth Maakah saves her city and her own life by taking the initiative in a time of danger and turmoil. She makes a difference.

I learned firsthand the powerful results that can come from taking initiative when I was in my late twenties and attending a small church of about three hundred members. A teenage girl in the church had contracted an autoimmune deficiency that had progressed to the point of making her bedridden, and the family was struggling to deal with their daughter's seemingly hopeless condition. The heartbreaking situation moved me to start a volunteer prayer program in which church members signed up to visit with the family and pray for healing for the young girl. I got enough volunteers to have one visit set up for almost every day of the week.

On the surface, I was certainly not the best choice to start this ministry. I was young, had only a casual connection with the family, and knew basically nothing about praying for physical healing. Yet I took the initiative to begin the ministry, and the body of Christ and the Holy Spirit took over from there. The family was greatly encouraged by the visits, and the young girl received healing, eventually returning to health and getting married. This experience taught me the power of initiative—God works and extends His kingdom through His chosen people stepping out to do His will.

The potential of initiative as part of a passionate Christian life cannot be underestimated. But we don't have to aspire to become an icon to initiate in God's kingdom. I've often found that most of God's plans seem to simply require someone willing to be a pioneer. So step out in faith by taking the initiative and watch God work!

06: NONCONFORMITY

DEFYING THE CROWD

Growing up in the 1980s, I experienced a decade that has been described as an era of consumption, optimism, individualism, and excess. Boasting such innovations as rap music, the Sony Walkman, MTV, cell phones, celebrity activism, and personal computers, the 1980s was a decade in which new ideas in technology, fashion, and finance were celebrated and pursued. Originality was the order of the day, and everyone tried to stand out from the crowd. I can't claim to have been much of a nonconformist during my youth, but I can vouch for the seismic effect of the Sony Walkman in my own life: my parents and I began actually getting along once I could listen to my own music in the car!

Nonconformity in America has a history that began long before the 1980s. The American colonies were founded by people unafraid to be different: enterprising speculators seeking their fortunes in Virginia, religious separatists launching holy communities in Massachusetts, and early human right activists welcoming people of every creed and nation in Rhode Island. Mary Easty was one early American nonconformist who maintained her convictions in the face of both intense pressure and personal physical danger. Easty was a fifty-eight-year-old married mother of seven when the witch trials began in Salem, Massachusetts, in 1692. Although she was an upstanding citizen and church member, Easty was accused of being a witch in the hysteria that followed, a nightmare that ultimately claimed twenty-four lives. At the time, if arrested, the surest way to escape conviction as a witch, although perhaps counterintuitive to modern minds, was to plead guilty to witchcraft. Although the charge of witchcraft would follow one for the duration of life, confessed witches were released from prison and not prosecuted, being seen as repentant and thus potentially capable of returning to the faith. Fifty-five persons accused of witchcraft during the hysteria confessed, but not Mary Easty.[1] Instead, she maintained her innocence and was convicted and hanged as a witch, but only after she had written a moving appeal to her judges in which she declares, "The Lord alone, who is the searcher of all hearts, knows that as I shall answer it at the tribunal seat, that I know not the least thing of witchcraft, therefore I cannot, I durst not belie my own soul."[2]

The pressure to confess must have been enormous. Boston merchant Robert Calef describes the strain on the accused in his 1700 history of the trials:

Besides that powerful argument, of life … there are numerous instances, too many to be here inserted, of the tedious examinations before private persons, many hours together; they all that time urging them to confess (and taking turns to persuade them) till the accused were wearied out by being forced to stand for so long, or for want of sleep.… But that which did mightily further such confessions, was their nearest and dearest relations urging them to it.… Hence it was that the husbands of some, by counsel often urging, and utmost earnestness, and children upon their knees entreating, have at length prevailed with them, to say they were guilty.[3]

Can you imagine the overwhelming onslaught of family and friends, ministers and justices that assailed Easty, urging her to confess? Or the intense strain of her own very human fear of death and suffering? I am amazed that she was able to stay strong in her refusal to lie before God. Also remarkable is that Easty's written appeal actually does not ask pardon for herself, but only for others: "I petition to your honours not for my own life, for I know I must die, and my appointed time is set; but … that no more innocent blood be shed, which undoubtedly cannot be avoided in the way and course you go in."[4] Calef reports that Easty's last farewell at her hanging was powerful, "drawing tears from the eyes of almost all present."[5] Her fortitude at her death as well as her poignant appeal may have moved hearts—Easty and the seven others who were hanged on September 22, 1692, were the last to die, as Governor William Phipps forbade additional imprisonments for witchcraft on October 12, beginning the termination of the hysteria. Easty's refusal to conform and lie before God may have saved many additional lives in this early battle for truth in the New World. Over time, nonconformity would come to be seen by many as a particularly American trait.

As Christians, we are called to be nonconformists in the sense of Paul's admonition in Romans 12:2: "Do not conform to the pattern of this world." Since we have chosen to follow Christ through the small gate on the narrow road of Matthew 7:14, we will be different from the unsaved world—a bright light that disdains the bushel, a city that is conspicuous on a hill, a holy nation that boldly reflects the remarkable news of God's love and grace for all humanity. We should stand out from the crowd.

Being different, however, is not always easy, and followers of God throughout the ages have struggled to maintain the courage and discretion necessary to resist conformity in a godly way. Believing you are in the right helps, having others at your side can bolster you, but sometimes you just have to take a stand alone. We have the promise of God that He will never forsake us, even if everyone turns against us, and we know we are more secure with Him than anywhere else: "Fear of man will prove to be a snare, but whoever trusts in the Lord is kept safe."[6] Times of nonconformity require us to lean even more deeply into the arms of our loving Father.

Even more challenging are the occasions when the path on which the Lord leads us differs even from that of other believers. These moments are probably the hardest for most Christians. In Mary Easty's case, her accusers were members of her own church. Like Easty, we are sometimes surprised when other believers question our decisions or beliefs, but it does happen. Have you ever stood in faith for a promise from God that your Christian friends suggested you abandon? Have you continued to minister to someone other believers labeled a lost cause? Have you persisted in asserting the truth of God's written word when other church members have dismissed it as irrelevant? Have you resisted a temptation your fellow Bible study members have deemed harmless? Christians aren't perfect, just forgiven, as the old saying goes, and there will be times in our lives when the path God leads us on will require us to deviate even from others with whom we fellowship. Only one leper in Luke 17 came back to thank Jesus for healing him while the other nine went on their way, and that leper was commended by Jesus for his faith.[7] We are each called to follow the Lord according to His desires for us personally.

How can having the strength to resist the crowd and follow what we know to be God's call upon our lives bolster our spiritual passion? First, it enables us to stand firm in our faith despite others' doubts. Mary Magdalene and the other women who had seen Jesus' empty tomb declared his resurrection, even when confronted with the disciples' disbelief.[8] Perhaps you have experienced an answer to prayer that some said would never come.

Second, nonconformity celebrates who we are as individuals in Christ. Our preciousness as unique creations of a perfect God is affirmed when we stand as individual representatives of God's calling and purpose. Jesus' mother Mary certainly went against the grain of her Jewish family and community by accepting God's call that she bear the Messiah, but her faith and steadfastness were rewarded and future generations have honored her. Maybe you have followed a call from God that led you to choose a path different from the one your parents, friends, or pastor believed was right for you, only to find that your choice led you to the destiny tailor-made for you by a loving Father.

Third, a willingness to resist the majority when necessary encourages us to embrace new, perhaps unconventional, ideas. At a time when the early church believed the salvation of God was only for the Jews, Peter was shown by God in a vision that Gentiles could be part of God's family as well. When Peter saw the reality of his vision played out days later in the conversion of the Roman centurion Cornelius, Peter adjusted his thinking on a core theological issue, admitting, "I now realize how true it is that God does not show favoritism but

accepts from every nation the one who fears him and does what is right."[9] Peter
then brought his realization of God's inclusive plan of salvation to the rest of
the Jewish believers in Jerusalem who had not thought such a thing was possible. Peter's break with convention effectively exploded an accepted doctrine of
the early church. Nonconformity, then, allows the passionate Christian to stand
firm despite the doubts of others, to affirm our own uniqueness in Christ, and to
accept innovative ideas when others cannot break from tradition.

But being a nonconformist can be tricky for Christians—how can I tell if I
am pursuing God's path for me without compromising or simply being stubborn
or rebellious? Quite simply, nonconformity that increases our passion for God
comes from the Holy Spirit only, not our own sinful desires to simply buck the
system, abandon the world to its sinfulness, tear down established traditions, get
ourselves noticed, or rebel against leaders or individuals whom we dislike or dis-
respect. Only by examining our hearts carefully under the direction of the Holy
Spirit can we determine that we are following the path of the Holy Spirit and not
one of our own devising. An attitude check can help us identify our motives: Do
we become unusually angry when others criticize our chosen path? Are we judg-
mental and critical of those who choose a different way? Do we spend an inordi-
nate amount of time trying to convince those around us that we are right? We may
be pursuing our own personal agenda if these statements are true of us.

On the contrary, when we are resisting conformity in a godly way, we will
be firm in our personal commitment, but will also continue to evidence love,
humility, and grace toward others, as Paul recommends in both Romans 14 and
1 Corinthians 8. We will not resort to anger, judgment, or condemnation, but we
will bear with others with patience and kindness, always seeking God's best for
them and forgiving their offenses toward us. It is helpful to remember that we
are not just individuals; we are each part of humanity as well as the worldwide
body of Christ, and love is always our highest calling. Although we may differ
in the details of what God requires of each of us, we should consistently "make
every effort to do what leads to peace and to mutual edification."[10] A sincere,
unfailing attitude of love and humility ensures godly, healthy nonconformity,
and the heroine of this chapter exemplifies this beautifully.

AN UNEXPECTED DINNER GUEST

Have you ever had to attend an event hosted by someone you were pretty
sure didn't like you? Miserable, isn't it? Yes, the rudiments of courtesy are observed, and nothing overtly unpleasant is said or done, but the whole experience
is blatantly uncomfortable. Jesus is faced with just such a situation in Luke 7
when he is invited to dinner at the home of Simon the Pharisee.[11] The Jewish
religious leaders of Jesus' day, the Pharisees were cynical at best about Jesus'

authenticity and ministry, and they often looked for opportunities to grill Him on sticky theological issues or entrap Him into saying something contradictory. Although the dinner invitation is probably just another attempt to challenge and discredit His character and ministry, Jesus is not one to resist an opportunity to share the good news of the Father, so He goes willingly.

Things don't start off well. Jesus is not given the customary kiss of greeting when He enters the room, He is not offered water to clean His feet after traveling on dusty roads, and He is not given oil to anoint His head. But the evening goes from bad to worse when a woman from the town who has "lived a sinful life," according to Luke, enters the room uninvited and begins weeping at Jesus' feet.[12] She then proceeds to wet His feet with her tears, dry them with her unbound hair, and kiss them, concluding her unexpected performance by anointing Jesus' feet with costly perfume from an alabaster jar. It is a startling public act of love, respect, and humility and is in direct contrast to the cool reception Jesus has been enduring from Simon and his guests.

The woman in this story is a nonconformist. In fact, our heroine has spent possibly her entire adult life suffering the very real repercussions of not conforming. Relegated to the outskirts of the community because of her sinful lifestyle, she knows what it means to go against the crowd. Derision, isolation, and grief have undoubtedly been her daily experience. Living with her own sense of shame and the judgment of others is her reality.

The dinner guests, on the other hand, are stalwart members of the community. They believe they are following the commands of God by testing Jesus, keeping Him at arms' length, working to entrap Him if necessary and prove that He is a false prophet. Their stance of icy, clinical interest tinged with suspicion is the perfect response to a self-proclaimed prophet from Nazareth who may be a serious danger to the spiritual well-being of God's people. Even Simon, who has extended only the most basic of courtesies as Jesus' host, disdains Jesus for accepting the woman and draws the hasty conclusion that He must not be a true prophet.

Who is following the way of God in this scenario? The sinful woman who defies convention and common sense by recklessly dumping costly perfume and her own dignity at the feet of a traveling minister? Or the dinner guests and their host who remain detached and guarded in their fortresses of pride and self-righteousness, reserving judgment until they are completely convinced? Jesus gives the nod to the woman when He shares with the company a story of two men whose debts to a moneylender were forgiven. At the end of the tale, Jesus asks Simon which man loved the moneylender more, and Simon answers that certainly the man who had owed more money loved the moneylender more. Jesus agrees, and goes on to rebuke Simon for his lack of true civility and respect during the evening, while commending the woman for her faith and love. Jesus warns His listeners that "whoever has been forgiven little loves little," before He forgives the woman and sends her on her way.[13] I'm pretty sure the roasted chicken was growing cold on the table as every eye in the room was riveted by such an unexpected, unusual event.

STEP 1: MAKING SACRIFICES

To be honest, this story is my favorite in all the New Testament. I simply cannot imagine the strength and humility it took for that woman to walk uninvited into a roomful of people who she knew would immediately judge her and possibly throw her out, and offer such an intimate act of love and adoration to a man who might do the very same. We do not know what precipitated her actions—had she heard Jesus preach, had she seen him performing miracles, had she been in the crowd one day when Jesus ministered to a leper or a prostitute? Whatever moved this woman, she is willing to go against the grain in a strikingly public way to show Jesus her love and gratitude. In doing so, our heroine reveals two important keys to godly, powerful, effective nonconformity—the willingness to sacrifice and the ability to move beyond boundaries.

The topic of sacrifice is never popular, of course. No one grows up hoping their life will hold lots and lots of sacrifices. But nonconformity requires lots and lots of sacrifices. As we can see from our story, the first sacrifice the woman has to make is her pride. Despite her lowly position in the community, she still certainly does not want to put herself in a position where she will experience further embarrassment and rejection. I can imagine her thoughts as she stands outside the door of Simon's house: "What will the guests think if a woman of my position dares to enter the home of a religious leader? Will Jesus draw back from my touch? Will I be thrown out before I even reach him? Perhaps I should just keep to myself and protect what little self-respect and dignity I have." Entering that room and performing her act of love and worship to Jesus must have been difficult in the extreme.

Our heroine sacrifices not only how she appears to others, but something that is precious and valuable to her in the real world—her alabaster jar of perfume. Such perfume was more expensive than oil and often required that the neck of the bottle be broken to access the contents. There was not really an option to pour out just a few drops and save the rest for later. The alabaster jar represents our heroine's total commitment to her act of worship—she offers her all to Jesus, regardless of cost. Surely some of the dinner guests lamented the "waste" of the perfume just as Judas Iscariot would later do when Mary of Bethany anoints Jesus' feet in the same way before His crucifixion.[14] But nonconformity always has a cost. As King David asserts in 2 Samuel 24:24b when building an altar to the Lord: "I will not sacrifice to the Lord my God burnt offerings that cost me nothing."

Lastly, the woman sacrifices her "right" to expect of others the same act of devotion to Jesus that she showed. She certainly could have decried the dinner guests' dispassionate reception of Jesus and defended her act of worship, but we do not read that she did. Instead, Jesus defended her. When we are called to walk a different path, we must always resist the temptation to judge or speak critically of those who disapprove of us. Our concern should be only with ourselves and our obedience to God. When Jesus told the disciple Peter the kind of death he would experience as a leader of the church, Peter inquired about God's plans for the disciple John. Jesus rebuked Peter by remarking, "If I want him to remain alive until I return, what is that to you? You must follow me."[15] We must always look to ourselves and acknowledge that the Holy Spirit leads each of us in His own way.

One woman who understood the sacrifices necessary to resist the crowd wrote these words about a very divisive topic in American history—African slavery:

> Have you considered, my children, the full amount of the evils of slavery? No, they cannot be seen by human powers. They form a part of those hidden things of darkness, which are linked by a chain which reaches into the dominion of Satan.[16]

Ann Page, born into wealth and privilege in Virginia in 1781, became mistress of more than two hundred slaves upon her marriage at the age of eighteen. After she became a Christian, Page grew distressed by slavery, but as a female in those times, she did not have the power to release her husband's slaves. Instead, Page committed herself to minister to the slaves, running a school for the young, visiting those who were sick, offering religious instruction to all, and closely monitoring her portion of the family finances to ensure that no slaves would have to be sold to pay debts. She even stopped the practice of dining out with friends for a time to spend those afternoons ministering to the slaves on her property. In a letter to one of her husband's overseers, Page remarks, "I dare not before God keep back from serving them in every way in my power. I shall soon be called to meet them at the judgment-seat of my Lord and Master."[17]

Sadly, one of the greatest trials Page suffered throughout her life was the judgment of those around her who disagreed with her choice to minister to those in slavery. She was criticized for a lack of judgment and discretion and was accused of jeopardizing the harmony of her community. Page records the struggles she experienced as she tried to show God's love to those who opposed and slandered her:

Am I in bonds of Christian love with every one? If I cannot clear up all my doings to the satisfaction of some, am I yet watching and praying that my spirit bears them nothing but tender love? If I cannot give up my judgment [that slavery is wrong], and act as some near and dear to me desire, am I maintaining my grounds in as gentle though firm a manner, as I should do, looking to Thee to give them light, or, if *I* am in error, to enlighten me?[18]

Page ultimately released her slaves after her husband's death, dying herself in 1838. Ann Page, like our heroine, was willing to sacrifice her reputation, her resources, and her desire to defend herself to others in her commitment to resist conformity.

STEP 2: MOVING BEYOND BOUNDARIES

While the willingness to sacrifice is a key part of godly nonconformity, the ability to move beyond boundaries is also important. Nonconformity is, by definition, a resistance to limits; it is a willingness to move beyond what others have determined are the acceptable confines of a situation. But our God does not accept conventional boundaries. He is a God of the impossible, not the possible. He is constantly pushing the envelope, encouraging us to go further, to try new things, to become something we never imagined we could be. He is always looking to do *more* than what we can envision, not just meet expectations. Think of the last time the Lord worked powerfully in your life. Weren't you surprised by the solution He came up with, the changes He effected in your heart, or the negative repercussions He enabled you to avoid? He is always working in ways that explode limits. As His followers, can we do any less? Can we willingly settle for what our eyes see and what the world tells us is possible? As Paul encourages us in Colossians 2:20, "Since you died with Christ to the elemental spiritual forces of this world, why, as though you still belonged to the world, do you submit to its rules?" Our heritage in Christ frees us from submitting to what is humanly possible. We don't have to live that way. Nonconformity allows us to follow God as He moves beyond the boundaries of this world, accomplishing His reckless, amazing, unimaginable plans and purposes.

Our heroine chooses to defy boundaries, and she does so in a way that is remarkable. First, her nonconformity is extravagant. She cries enough tears to fill a wash basin, ignores both stench and dirt as well as social convention by using her unbound hair to wipe Jesus' dirty feet, lavishes Him with kisses, and pours her own perfume upon His feet. Everything that Simon the host has neglected to offer Jesus, she gives Him in spades. Ground water from the well is not good enough for Jesus—He must have her own tears of repentance and love to wash His feet. A quick kiss of greeting on the cheek will not do—He deserves the honor of heartfelt affection bestowed on Him ceaselessly. A drop of oil on the head is inadequate—only perfume from an alabaster jar is worthy of Jesus. This woman knows the truth of the statement that those who have been forgiven little, love little before Jesus even shares the parable. The forgiveness and love God bestows on us goes so far beyond our human understanding that nothing we can offer Him in this life can be too much. Our heroine embodies this truth as she moves beyond boundaries in a way that is intentionally excessive.

Another interesting characteristic of the woman's rejection of boundaries is that her act is purely physical. It is directed toward Jesus' human body and is performed by the woman's body. The dirt, dust, and stench are physically removed from Jesus as the woman kneels, kisses, cries, anoints, and dries. We are not told her thoughts during this episode, and Luke does not record that she says one word. Placing myself in her shoes, I'm fairly certain my first action would have been to launch into a hurried explanation of why I had come, or a lengthy apology for disturbing the dinner party, or a hasty offer to meet Jesus at some time more convenient for Him. I doubt I would have let my actions do all the talking!

Our Christian culture is an extremely verbal one. We are admitted to church membership or baptism on the basis of how well we can relate a personal testimony, we are given a seminary degree if we can articulate practical and theological truths related to our faith, and we follow with eager interest those leaders who can deliver a stimulating address before a crowd. Certainly we should seek to be winsomely articulate regarding the truths of our faith and personal experience, but, without a doubt, actions speak louder than words, and actions are physical. When Paul defends his apostleship in 1 Corinthians 4, he urges his readers to emulate his "way of life in Christ Jesus, which agrees with what I teach everywhere in the church." His authority as an apostle of Christ is validated by his actions, for "the kingdom of God is not a matter of talk but of power."[19]

I urge you to consider the physical aspect of your relationship with God. Is He calling you to *do* something new and different? Consider joining a ministry at your church that involves physical service, like working with special needs children or running errands for the elderly. Adopt a different physical position during corporate worship or your personal prayer times.[20] When I attend churches that are more physically demonstrative in worship than my own, I seek to experience God in new ways by raising my hands, dancing, or lying prostrate. Try fasting from food, forgoing sleep for a night of prayer, or training for a local run to raise money for a charitable cause. Donning a medieval hair shirt might be a bit extreme, but bringing our physical bodies into our spiritual lives in new ways can create unique opportunities for growth in our hearts and minds in ways that move us beyond our own boundaries.

Finally, our heroine moves beyond boundaries with actions that are intensely personal. She does not write a check to Jesus' ministry or add a positive comment to His blog—she comes to Him personally and interacts with Him in a deeply intimate way. It is a mystery of Christianity that we are each personally and intimately connected to Christ and His mission through the power of the Holy Spirit in our hearts. Paul repeatedly makes this point in his letters, with statements such as the following:

> We always carry around in our body the death of Jesus, so that the life of Jesus may also be revealed in our body. (2 Cor. 4:10)

> Now if we are children, then we are heirs—heirs of God and co-heirs with Christ, if indeed we share in his sufferings in order that we may also share in his glory. (Rom. 8:17)

> I want to know Christ—yes, to know the power of his resurrection and participation in his sufferings, becoming like him in his death, and so, somehow, attaining to the resurrection from the dead. (Phil. 3:10, 11)

> For just as we share abundantly in the sufferings of Christ, so also our comfort abounds through Christ. (2 Cor. 1:5)

In fact, Paul contends that his ministry is so intimately connected to the work of Jesus that it continues what Jesus did not finish on earth: "Now I rejoice in what I am suffering for you, and I fill up in my flesh what is still lacking in regard to Christ's afflictions, for the sake of his body, which is the church."[21] David makes this point as well in Psalm 69:

> For I endure scorn for your sake,
>   and shame covers my face.
> I am a foreigner to my own family,
>   a stranger to my own mother's children;
> for zeal for your house consumes me,
>   and the insults of those who insult you fall on me. (Ps. 69:7–9)

What is this startlingly intimate connection between God and His people? Frail and human though we are, we share both the glory and sufferings of our perfect God. We bring heaven's reality to the world in such a way as to become to God the Father "the pleasing aroma of Christ among those who are being saved and those who are perishing."[22] This deep, personal connection with the God we serve and adore will force us to push the boundaries, to stand out, to be different. We cannot do otherwise. Our heroine understands that, and her very personal act of devotion moves Jesus' heart.

RECEIVING GOD'S BLESSINGS

A willingness to sacrifice and to move beyond boundaries produces a nonconformity that accomplishes God's purposes, and we are blessed by the fruit of our choices. The woman in our story gives Jesus all she has in contrast to those around her, and she receives back an abundance of blessings. Certainly the first blessing we notice is that Jesus forgives her sins and commends her love and faith. Her extreme act of devotion releases her from the bondage of her sin and she can now "go in peace."[23] Contrast this reality with the experience of the dinner guests—their cool, calculated response to Jesus leaves them still in need of forgiveness and restoration. We can only hope that some of them eventually followed her example.

The woman also receives from Jesus a new direction for her life. By forgiving her sins, Jesus negates her old way of life and sets her on a path that is new and hopeful. When we step out and resist conformity, we often experience opportunities that we would not have received if we had remained with the crowd. She is the only person in our story who begins a new journey that evening. She is the only one who will wake up the next morning with hope for a different, more promising, more exciting future. Breaking with the crowd and following God's call opens up a world of possibilities for us.

Lastly, our heroine receives revelation from God when Jesus reveals His authority to forgive sins in response to her act of worship. We have no record that Simon's questioning of Jesus or the dinner table conversation elicited such a revelation. God reveals His truth to those who seek Him in sincerity. It is ironic that the dinner guests, most of whom probably knew the Old Testament scriptures backwards and forwards, planned to quiz Jesus to learn more about Him, but it was the one person who chose instead a path of love and gratitude who discovered the most about Him. As Romans 12:2 promises, "Do not conform to the pattern of this world, but be transformed by the renewing of your mind. *Then* you will be able to test and approve what God's will is—His good, pleasing and perfect will" (emphasis added). The woman's nonconformity leads her to a deeper understanding of Jesus.

Nonconformity will look different for each of us, but its essence is a willingness to sacrifice and defy boundaries when we are called by God to follow the road less traveled. Our passion for God is stoked when we have the courage to pursue His path for us, regardless of how that route breaks with patterns that may be familiar, appealing, or time-honored. As passionate Christians, we must become comfortable with going against the crowd because we will undoubtedly stand out in our pursuit of God and His purposes. But the blessings we will receive as passionate nonconformists will be beyond our wildest dreams.

07: TENACITY

BREAKING THROUGH BARRIERS

At the 2012 Summer Olympic Games in London, one of the most eagerly anticipated rivalries was the battle between American swimmers Michael Phelps and Ryan Lochte. Strong competitors with opposite personalities outside the pool, both swimmers had earned numerous Olympic medals over their remarkably successful careers. After competing in various events throughout the Olympics, Phelps and Lochte met in the finals of the two-hundred-meter individual medley (200 IM). Lochte had beaten Phelps in the 200 IM at the 2010 U.S. Nationals and again at the 2011 World Championships, but both races had been close. The London 200 IM did not disappoint. This time, Phelps edged out Lochte to win the gold medal.

The extraordinary improbability of this Olympic rivalry between Lochte and Phelps in the 200 IM was a fact probably not known to most of the spectators that day. Before defeating Phelps in the 200 IM in 2010, Lochte had lost to Phelps seventeen straight times, beginning in 2002. Seventeen straight losses over an eight-year period! I probably would have given up after the first race! But Lochte persevered, pushing himself to improve, and crediting Phelps with making him into a champion swimmer: "He pushes me every day. And I push him."[1]

We are impressed when someone has the tenacity to keep trying after seventeen straight failures because tenacity seems to be in short supply in our culture. Perhaps more than any other attribute discussed in this book, real tenacity is hard to find. We give up on our debts, relationships, jobs, dreams, New Year's resolutions, and summer diets without a second thought. Can you think of someone in your immediate circle of friends and acquaintances who would continue to persevere after coming up short seventeen times? Would you?

Why is it so hard for us to resist giving up? The reasons are as numerous as they are varied. Laziness, fear, boredom, hopelessness, desire for security, reluctance to appear weak or to take risks—countless emotions can play a part in destroying our willingness to persevere. Tenacity is demanding because it requires putting our heart into what we are pursuing, and putting our heart into anything requires courage and strength and makes us vulnerable to failure, rejection, loss, and pain. Too often, it seems that despite our best intentions, we simply cannot sustain the battle.

But tenacity is necessary for us to grow and thrive. It helps us push through the barriers in our lives—emotional, physical, even spiritual obstacles that block our forward progress. Yes, we've lost seventeen straight times, but we might win the next one if we continue to fight! Tenacity moves us beyond these barriers by switching our focus from the current setback to the future possibility of success. It gives our passion one more opportunity to reach fulfillment.

Psychologist Angela Lee Duckworth of the University of Pennsylvania studied people as varied as West Point cadets, National Spelling Bee participants, inner-city middle school students, and up-and-coming salespeople to determine what produces success. Who would succeed, and who would fail? The one factor that emerged in all her studies as the only "significant predictor" of future success is what she calls "grit," defined by Duckworth as "passion and perseverance for very long-term goals." According to Duckworth, "Our data showed very clearly that there are many talented individuals who simply do not follow through on their commitments. In fact, in our data, grit is usually unrelated or even inversely related to measures of talent."[2] Tenacity can be more important than ability, experience, or even resources in moving us toward success.

When I told a close friend of mine that I was writing about the quality of tenacity, she laughed and responded, "You're the perfect person to write about tenacity. That's your middle name!" Deep down, of course, I wished that she had identified exemplary spirituality, remarkable intelligence, or overall awesomeness as my defining character trait. But, actually, she might be right. I am not usually the most gifted or talented person in the room, but I seldom give up on a goal. My experience in graduate school revealed to me the importance of tenacity. I will never forget my first day in a graduate seminar, my eyes roving from face to face, my ears hoping they would soon hear something they actually understood. Was I really this unprepared for graduate studies in literature, I wondered sadly? I couldn't even understand the vocabulary the other students were using, let alone the theoretical concepts they were discussing. Could I ever catch up? Well, it turns out I could catch up, but only if I worked hard. Despite being certainly the least brilliant member of my class, I finished my degree before most of my fellow students, simply because I refused to lose sight of my goal. Tenacity is indispensable in helping us move past barriers in our lives to accomplish the goals we seek.

But not everyone is instinctively tenacious. How can we develop this attribute if it doesn't come naturally to us?

The heroine of our story in this chapter is tenacious, to say the least, and we can learn from her how to grow in this attribute. She perseveres toward her goal to help her suffering child despite a husband who is nonexistent, a society that is dismissive, and a band of foreigners who are discriminatory. How does she resist giving up in the face of such barriers?

LOOKING FOR LOVE IN ALL THE WRONG PLACES

Our story begins with exasperation. Serious exasperation. New Testament writers Matthew and Mark record that Jesus is ministering to the Jews in Galilee, and His fame is growing. However, no one seems to understand His message. Both the Jewish religious leaders and Jesus' own disciples continue to believe their right standing with God is based on obedience to human traditions and their bloodlines as Jews. Jesus' focus on obedience from the heart and sincere faith is going unheeded.[3] Frustrated, Jesus advises those listening to His teachings to abandon the Jewish religious leaders, for they are "blind guides."[4] His disappointment extends to His disciples, whom He also chastises: "'Are you still so dull?' Jesus asked them. 'Don't you see that whatever enters the mouth goes into the stomach and then out of the body? But the things that come out of a person's mouth come from the heart, and these defile them.'"[5] It appears that Jesus' call to a life of authentic relationship with God and heart obedience are falling on deaf ears.

After this episode, Jesus leaves Hebrew territory and travels north of Galilee to the Gentile city of Tyre. Heavily influenced by Greek culture, Tyre had a history of Canaanite pagan worship. Jesus attempts to retire to a private home in the area to escape the crowds, but He is discovered, and one person who seeks Him out is a Syrophoenician woman whose young daughter is suffering from demon possession. "Lord, Son of David," the woman cries to Jesus, "have mercy on me! My daughter is demon-possessed and suffering terribly."[6] According to Matthew, the woman keeps up her pleas for mercy until the disciples grow weary of her wailing and urge Jesus to ask her to leave.

We have in this story a picture of a mother facing extremely daunting barriers as she seeks a solution to her daughter's suffering. Her Hellenistic culture cannot offer a cure, and many of her friends (and perhaps even her family) have probably distanced themselves due to her daughter's off-putting ailment. Also significant is the lack of a husband's presence, particularly in this society; apparently, this woman is alone in her attempts to help her child. We can imagine the loneliness and hopelessness of her struggle.

Desperate, our heroine decides to approach those whom she hopes will accept and help her—a Jewish preacher who teaches the importance of love and his faithful followers. Despite the fact that they are foreigners, they have a reputation for healing and caring. Unfortunately, the disciples do not live up to this reputation. Rather than embodying the kindness and mercy of the God of Israel, they show her no sympathy whatsoever. Instead, frustrated that the woman "keeps crying out after [them]," the disciples use their influence to entreat Jesus to "send her away."[7] Sadly, our heroine will not find the solution to her problem among even the closest followers of Jesus.

Have you experienced barriers like the ones this mother faces? Chronic physical suffering, spiritual struggles, lack of support, marital difficulties, judgment from others, rejection, hopelessness, despair? There are many people and circumstances arrayed against her, and now even Jesus' disciples are rejecting her. Yet, somehow, she perseveres. What gives her the tenacity to continue pursuing help for her child?

Our heroine has two things going for her: a strong incentive to persevere and a close connection to Jesus. How do these two realities help her resist giving up? First, our mother is just that—a mother. And, as a mother, she is super-motivated to fight for her goal of seeing her daughter healed. And it is a worthy goal. If we are having trouble persevering, the first step is to ask ourselves if the goal we are seeking is truly worth it. If not, then abandon the battle and move on to a fight that matters. Second, our heroine makes another choice that is key to tenacity: she remains close to Jesus. I can imagine her skirting around the edges of Jesus' entourage, always keeping Him in sight and within earshot. Why is this choice important? To put it simply, pursuing a challenging goal can be draining and often painful, and spending time with the Lord provides a wholeness and strength that can only come from Him. As David writes in Psalm 16:11: "You will fill me with joy in your presence." Time in God's presence is necessary to strengthen us to be tenacious, and it's a great place to start if you are struggling in your battle to persevere.

If you are currently facing a situation that requires persevering for the long haul, consider setting aside fifteen minutes a day to let your heart rest in God's presence. Spend no time on the situation you are currently facing. Don't pray about it, don't obsess over it, don't attempt to discover ways to solve it. Those activities are for another time. In this fifteen minutes, focus your energy solely on connecting with God and bringing your spirit to rest in His presence. Listen to worship music, enjoy the silence, take a meditative walk, or perhaps memorize and meditate on God's promise of care for you from Psalm 91:4:

> He will cover you with his feathers,
> and under his wings you will find refuge;
> his faithfulness will be your shield and rampart.

Your goal in this time is to be near to Jesus like our heroine was. Being with the Lord is such a blessing and privilege that nothing else needs to be accomplished to validate the time spent. Like our heroine, we can leverage our motivation for persevering and our intimacy with God to sustain our tenacity in the face of obstacles.

ENCOUNTERING GOD'S SILENCE

One of the best things about being a Christian is that even if others reject us, we can always turn to God for acceptance and love. Well, except for those times when He's not answering us. Have you ever encountered a period of God's silence? Disheartening, isn't it? We feel as though we are talking to the ceiling—asking for mercy, pleading for direction, craving kindness that does not appear to be forthcoming. The scriptural promises of God's unending, unconditional love and concern for us appear rather hollow and empty indeed, and feelings of betrayal and confusion are often the result. Even worse, times of God's silence can deal a death blow to our desire to persevere. How do we understand and navigate those challenging times?

My husband Steve and I were one of those unhappy couples who struggled to conceive children. Despite several years of trying, and various medical approaches, we were still childless and answerless. We had no assurance from God that we would one day be parents, no answer for why we were struggling, and no real sense of direction on how to proceed. That was a difficult time, as we watched our friends start families with apparent ease, while we had little hope and even less understanding. However, one day, after beginning a new medical treatment, I was spending time with God in prayer, and I felt an assurance in my spirit that I was pregnant. I immediately took a pregnancy test and can remember sinking against the wall in shock and emotion when I saw that it was positive. Our prayers had been answered!

But why the time of lengthy silence from God? I would love to share the secrets God revealed to me about His motives, but I can't say that I received any. This side of heaven, I may never know God's purposes for us during that season, but I can certainly attest to the struggle, questioning, and striving that those years of God's silence produced in me.

Our heroine experiences a similar "silent treatment" from Jesus. Matthew records in his narrative that despite the woman's constant cries for mercy, "Jesus did not answer a word."[8] What a simple sentence! So easy to write! So easy to read! So difficult to experience. Not a word of answer for a woman who is begging for healing for her child who is suffering at the hands of Satan? Doesn't the disciple John assert in 1 John 3:8 that the reason Jesus came to earth was to "destroy the devil's work"? Why not heal this woman's poor daughter and bring glory to the Father?

The question of God's silence during times of trial is certainly too profound and complex for one chapter in a book, but we do know some of the reasons God withholds His answers. The most obvious is that we may not be truly listening. Often, especially during times of intense emotional stress, our prayers can focus solely on having our needs met in the way we want, rather than honestly seeking God's heart and purposes for our situation. When I was praying for a child, was I really listening to God or was I simply repeating to Him my desires?

Sometimes, the reason may be timing. How did I change as a person during the years before God blessed us with a child? Was I now ready to parent in the way God needed me to, a way that I couldn't have years earlier?

Perhaps God's silence is designed to stoke our passion, our desire for His voice and ways. Even though the disciples do not care for the woman's unceasing pleas for mercy, one biblical commentator on our passage notes that Jesus values sustained, increasing passion in His children: "Continued importunity may be uneasy to men, even to good men; but Christ loves to be cried after."[9] Did my desire for intimacy with God increase as a result of my struggles with infertility?

Lastly, God's silence may be designed to reveal our hearts. What did I discover about myself through my struggle with God's silence? Could I have learned about the impatience and selfishness concealed in my heart in any other way?

Jesus confides to His disciples His reason for not answering the woman's plea: "I was sent only to the lost sheep of the house of Israel."[10] Clearly, it is not the woman's time to have her request answered. Although we know from other biblical passages that God's plan of salvation is for people throughout the entire world, at this time, Jesus is only directed to the Jews. God's silence is the answer this woman receives.

RESPONDING TO SILENCE

Our heroine, however, is not privy to Jesus' explanation of God the Father's timing in this situation, and her tenacity pushes her to continue to pursue Jesus despite His silence. She eventually falls at His feet in verse 25 of Matthew 15 and pleads, "Lord, help me!"

Jesus now breaks His silence and speaks to her. What has changed about the woman or her request? Did she just wear Jesus out with her pleading? I would suggest that simply more begging by the mother was not the reason Jesus answers her. I believe the woman makes two choices in the light of Jesus' silence that move the Lord's heart to speak to her. First, she bases her persistence on seeking His help solely on His character as Lord and Savior. Neither Matthew nor Mark records any negotiating by the woman. She does not offer Him a deal if He delivers her daughter from the demon that is torturing her, she does not begin recounting her own acts of righteousness, she does not attempt to argue the validity of her request. She simply relies on Jesus' nature as One who has both the power and compassion to heal. By calling Him "Lord" and "Son of David," this mother acknowledges Jesus' position of authority. Does she recognize that He is the Messiah? Some commentators say yes,[11] but regardless of the extent of her understanding, her reliance upon Jesus alone must have been a refreshing change from the Jews to whom Jesus had been ministering, who never failed to trumpet their own righteousness and bloodline in their demands for favor from God.

When we face times of God's silence, we must make a similar choice and focus on who God is as revealed in the Bible. His character will strengthen our resolve to persevere in the face of His silence. He is a God who loves us, forgives us and forgets our offenses, shows us kindness and mercy, and works all things for our good. He is not vindictive, punitive, petty, malicious, or tyrannical. He always acts toward us with love, even though we may not always understand His ways. When we recall the character of the God we serve and adore, our tenacity will be based on a firm foundation and will move the heart of God. Recounting Scripture passages that proclaim the reality of who God is, resisting the urge to "bargain" with God, and spending time in worship and praise are effective, practical ways to strengthen our tenacity and our spirits. Jesus breaks His silence when He sees that the woman relies only on who He is and not on anything she has to offer.

Second, the woman comes to Jesus in humility. This is a simple point, but a crucial one and a natural corollary to the point above. When we rely solely on God's character to give us perseverance in times of silence, we are acknowledging our own absolute lack of righteousness, and humility is the result. This mother falls on her knees at the feet of Jesus and begs, "Lord, help me!" Her physical position is humble and so is her request. Gone is her dignity and even the mention of her daughter. Her pleading has been reduced to kneeling before Jesus and asking simply, "Help me." Her humble attitude acknowledges Jesus' authority and power.

Our heroine's humility also enables her to resist complaining about Jesus' lack of response, blaming Him for her daughter's condition, or slandering His character. This is the true benefit of cultivating an attitude of humility during times of God's silence—it enables us to walk the fine line between expressing our hurt and anger to the Lord in a healthy way while avoiding criticizing or falsely accusing Him. On the one hand, there is nothing wrong with admitting our pain and exasperation to the Lord. The Bible is full of people like David who poured out to God the rage, grief, and frustration they experienced. But what we want to avoid when we are hurting is indulging in thoughts or words that attribute wrongdoing to Him in any way. God does not sin; every one of His choices is good, loving, and just. Thus, an attitude of humility while waiting on the Lord to speak not only saves us from moving toward accusation and criticism, but also keeps us in a place in which we can release our pain to God in a productive way and experience His strengthening love.

Letting go of our pain and anger to the Lord in a positive way can be tricky when our emotions are running high. I try to follow three steps when I feel the need to unburden myself to the Lord. First, I share honestly with Him how I am feeling, trying not to hide behind a façade of inappropriate self-reliance or false holiness. No matter how long it takes, I communicate everything I am feeling to Him. Next, I allow God to respond to my crying out. I wait for the Holy Spirit to bring to my mind a passage of Scripture, a worship song, an attribute of God—anything that He wants to share with me to remind me of His love and compassion. I spend some time in His presence, meditating on what He has shared with me, and allowing His love to heal my heart. Last, I spend time praising God for His care and love for me and for His perfect and unchangeable nature. I acknowledge, usually out loud, that my Father is always on my side and works all things for my good. I intentionally declare that He cares for me and loves me and will never forsake me. This final step helps me end these times with the Lord with an accurate perspective and with a feeling of hope. If you are struggling right now with releasing your pain to the Lord in a beneficial, healthy manner, consider trying these steps and seeing how they work for you.

The benefit of relying on God's character instead of our own righteousness and adopting an attitude of humility during periods of waiting on God is that we will eventually hear God's voice. Contrary to what we may begin to suspect, God does not stay silent forever. He is a God who loves to communicate with His children, and when we maintain an attitude of respect and humility during His silence, we are ready to hear what He has to say when He begins to speak. It reminds me of my younger son's days as a wide receiver on his school football team. On each play, he was expected to run his route in such a way that he ended up in the exact spot to which the quarterback was going to throw the ball. The quarterback didn't have time to watch my son run his route; he simply threw the ball to where my son was supposed to be at the end of the play. If my son was there, he caught the ball. If he was not, he caught something else from the coach! Relying on God's character and maintaining an attitude of humility places us in the position to hear God's voice when He chooses to speak. Our heroine is rewarded with Jesus' eventual attention and response—she finally hears the voice of the One she has sought after with remarkable tenacity.

HANDLING GOD'S ANSWER

The phrase "going from bad to worse" was not, to my knowledge, coined specifically for our heroine, but one could make a strong case that she could be its poster child. After ignoring the humble pleadings of this mother, Jesus finally answers her by disclosing the reason for His silence: "It is not right to take the children's bread and throw it to the dogs."[12] Ouch! Jesus essentially informs the woman that He cannot dispense the salvation and blessings of God that are designed for the Jewish people (children) to the pagan nations outside the Hebrew faith (dogs). Basically, this woman's ethnicity bars her from receiving deliverance from Jesus for her daughter. In fact, this is the only time in Jesus' recorded ministry that He refuses a request for healing. It should be noted that the word Jesus uses for "dogs" means beloved household pets, not stray mongrels, but His words certainly still sting. His rejection of her request appears to be final. Clearly, this is a barrier that even tenacity cannot break through.

But not so fast! Our heroine challenges Jesus with a response: "Yes, Lord, yet even the dogs eat the crumbs that fall from their master's table."[13] Wow! What an impressive comeback! It would have taken me weeks to conjure up that retort. Interestingly, Jesus does not miss a beat. "O woman, great is your faith! Be it done for you as you desire," He answers her, and Matthew records that her daughter is healed from that instant.[14] The beleaguered mother's tenacity pays off and her request of Jesus is granted.

Does the ending of this story surprise you? It surprises me. Jesus has just entered pagan territory and is quite clear in His remarks to both His disciples and the woman that He is not called to minister to the Gentiles at this point. However, by the end of the passage, He ends up not only granting our Syrophoenician heroine's request, but afterward traveling to the pagan city of Sidon and then farther into the region of the Decapolis, a league of ten cities unified by their Greek culture, where he heals a deaf and mute person and feeds a crowd of four thousand. His teachings and miracles continue in Gentile territory for what some commentators consider an entire year.[15]

I am also surprised at Jesus' response because I was always taught in church to accept "no" from God when I hear it. Why is this woman rewarded for her faith and tenacity by having her request granted after she refuses to accept Jesus' seemingly clear and final answer of no?

This woman's experience teaches us one very important lesson about the role of tenacity in developing spiritual passion: God expects us to use tenacity to recognize and seize the opportunities He offers us. Jesus' answer to our heroine is actually not a final refusal. By couching his response in a structure like an aphorism—a general truth presented in a concise, memorable manner—Jesus opens the door ever so slightly for the woman to respond in kind. And our heroine takes advantage of this opportunity, using Jesus' words to kick open the door even further: "Yes, Lord, I understand and accept that your mission is primarily to those of the house of Israel, but I will be happy with just the overflow of the immense blessing that you bring."

In reality, our heroine is in good company when she exhibits a tenacity that takes advantage of the opportunities God offers, even in the face of what looks like Jesus' refusal. Consider Abraham who pushed past God's decree that Sodom and Gomorrah would be destroyed, Moses who resisted God's plan to wipe out the Israelites when they refused to enter the Promised Land, and Jesus' own mother Mary who ignored her Son's direct refusal to perform a miracle when the wine ran out at the wedding they were attending at Cana.[16] Interestingly, Jesus' very first recorded miracle, turning water into wine at the wedding, was produced by his mother's tenacity despite Jesus' initial rejection of her request, again because it was ostensibly not the proper time. They were all, like our heroine, seeking mercy for others, a trademark of God Himself, and that desire for God to act according to His heart of love motivated them past His seeming refusal. Is it true that God is looking for believers who will tenaciously step through the small openings He offers and plead with Him to bless the world with His love and power?

In our story, the disciples are also told by Jesus that His ministry is only to the people of Israel, but they do not push past that answer like our heroine does. They do not remind Jesus of the Father's heart for the lost. They do not mention Yahweh's compassion for the lonely and hurting. They do not recite Old Testament scriptures such as Isaiah 56:3–8 or Psalm 2:8 that promise that God will be the Father of all the peoples on earth. And, most significantly, they do not think to apply the teaching they just received from Jesus days earlier before they entered Tyre on how true faith is not related to bloodline or following human rules. Certainly they recognize that Jesus would not contradict Himself! Is Jesus hoping that they will be tenacious enough to apply what they are learning from Him about God the Father and ask for mercy for the woman and her pagan neighbors despite Jesus' seeming refusal? Sadly, they do not. Instead, Jesus must hope that a Syrophoenician mother of a demon-possessed child will recognize the heart of a foreign God and persist in her request for healing after He makes the same statement to her. Happily, she does, and Jesus can then acknowledge her faith and act according to the Father's heart, delivering her daughter from demonic oppression and commencing His ministry of love and healing to the pagan nations around Him.

So does this mean that in our pursuit of a tenacious, passionate heart we are never to take no from God for an answer? No, I believe there are requests that God does not desire to grant, but the key for us at these times is to discover the new direction in which He wants us to go. He never wants to end the dialogue with a simple no. He always desires to both show us how to pray and to change our hearts. In our heroine's case, He wanted to see her heart of faith and hear her pronounce a spiritual truth that His disciples had consistently failed to grasp as He launched His ministry to the pagan nations. Perhaps He desired to give Sodom and Gomorrah a second chance and to make Abraham's heart soft for a sinful city as the soon-to-be patriarch inched toward fathering a great nation. Maybe Moses' commitment to the Israelites needed to be strengthened before he embarked on leading them for an additional forty years in the wilderness. Perhaps Mary needed to be the first to reveal faith in her Son as the Chosen One who had authority on earth to perform miracles. When we hear an answer of no from God, we must seek Him more earnestly. He wants to move us to a place in which we will not just pray His will, but also be changed by Him. Perhaps no is His final answer, but perhaps He is opening a different door for us to move through as well.

THE FRUIT OF TENACITY

Of course, the fruit our heroine receives from her perseverance in the face of numerous barriers is the granting of her request—her daughter is delivered and her faith is confirmed. Demonstrating tenacity has the dual benefit of changing our hearts and accomplishing God's will in our lives and the lives of others. And it is an indispensable quality for those who want to pursue the Lord with passion.

As lovers of Jesus, we are not cultivating tenacity to win Olympic gold medals. We are seeking a heavenly reward that is worth much more than any accomplishments we could receive here earth. As the apostle Paul exhorts us in 2 Corinthians 4:16–18:

> Therefore we do not lose heart. Though outwardly we are wasting away, yet inwardly we are being renewed day by day. For our light and momentary troubles are achieving for us an eternal glory that far outweighs them all. So we fix our eyes not on what is seen, but on what is unseen, since what is seen is temporary, but what is unseen is eternal.

Ask the Holy Spirit to help you take the next step toward exhibiting a tenacious, passionate spirit as you seek to follow Him.

08: GENEROSITY

OVERCOMING DESPAIR

Abby was a beautiful woman. Intelligent and wealthy, she had everything she could ever want—except a husband who loved her. Cruel, arrogant, and foolish, Abby's husband made her life miserable. Abby struggled with hopelessness and despair, fearing that she was doomed to a life of sadness and pain.

One day, Abby received word from her housekeeper that her husband had dishonestly broken a business deal with a very important person in their city, and that this person was now plotting to ruin the entire family. Quickly, Abby got online and sent a selection of gifts to the injured party, to be delivered immediately. Then she jumped into a taxi and headed to the man's office. Greeting him at his office door, Abby clasped his hand in a firm shake and blurted out her apologies for the arrogance of her husband. "I'm sorry that my husband treated you so disrespectfully," apologized Abby. "I know you are well respected and have a great future ahead of you in this city. As your business grows, I am certain that you will not want to find yourself entangled in any unsavory dealings with my husband simply for revenge. Please consider forgiving the matter and moving on." The man affirmed the wisdom of her advice and agreed.

Imagine the businessman's surprise when, a few weeks later, he heard that Abby's husband had died suddenly of a heart attack. Calling her to offer his condolences, the man ended up asking Abby to meet for dinner. They hit it off, and later married. The businessman continued to be successful, and they had a son. Abby was finally cherished and happy.

Perhaps you guessed the biblical story I am attempting to modernize—the first meeting of David and Abigail. Old Testament chronicler Samuel describes in 1 Samuel 25 how the future king of Israel, David, is wandering in the Desert of Maon with his six hundred men, trying to elude the soldiers of King Saul as they seek his life. David has been anointed king by the prophet Samuel, but has yet to assume the throne, and he is struggling with discouragement in the wake of Samuel's recent death, Saul's relentless quest to kill him, and his own delayed ascension as king. In an attempt to sustain his hungry fighting men, David sends messengers to Nabal, a wealthy man of the region who is holding a sheepshearing festival to celebrate the profits he expects from the sale of his wool. David instructs his men to remind Nabal that David and his followers had helped protect Nabal's flocks and shepherds while they were grazing in Carmel, and to ask Nabal to give them whatever portion he can spare. However, not only does Nabal refuse to give anything to David, he also insults him by retorting, "Who is this David? Who is this son of Jesse? Many servants are breaking away from their masters these days. Why should I take my bread and water, and the meat I have slaughtered for my shearers, and give it to men coming from who knows where?"[1]

Upon hearing Nabal's refusal to share the fruits of the labor, David swears revenge on Nabal's entire household, setting out with about four hundred of his men for Nabal's homestead. Nabal's wife Abigail, hearing of the impending attack from a servant, acts quickly and meets David with gifts and supplies as he approaches Nabal's property. Abigail assuages David's anger by first apologizing for Nabal's rudeness and then by reminding David that God will establish a lasting rule for him in Israel. Abigail encourages David to spare Nabal and thus save his own conscience from "the staggering burden of needless bloodshed."[2] Convinced of the wisdom of her words, David abandons his quest for revenge. Nabal dies by the Lord's hand ten days later, and David takes Abigail as his third wife. They will later have a son named Kileab.[3]

What an exciting story! Broken promises, avowed revenge, a desperate quest to avert disaster—these are the elements of a great feature film. Add in a beautiful, unappreciated heroine and a charismatic, dashing heir apparent, and you have your blockbuster. But underlying the excitement and suspense of this story is the painful subplot of Abigail's difficult life with her husband Nabal. The narrative identifies Nabal as "surly and mean," a servant calls him "wicked," and Abigail admits to David that Nabal is a "Fool."[4] Although we are not given many details about Nabal and Abigail's relationship, what we are told is disturbing and saddening, and it is not hard for us to imagine Abigail's sufferings. Painful relationships can create in us a sense of anger, shame, frustration, and even despair. Despair especially can be damaging to our emotional health and can block us from passionately pursuing God.

I can recall the despair I felt the first time I lost a close family member to death. I was a high school sophomore, and my maternal grandfather passed away suddenly in the night from a heart attack. If I close my eyes, I can still feel my parents waking me out of a dead sleep and packing us all into the car to make the two-hour drive to the hospital, only to find that he had already passed. My grandfather's unexpected death left me with a range of emotions, one of which was despair. I could not bring my grandfather back, assuage my mother and grandmother's pain, or stop death from eventually claiming other members of my family. That experience was my introduction to the hopelessness, frustration, and pain that despair can bring.

We can all recall situations that led us to a sense of despair, and the ensuing struggles with grief, uncertainty, or even depression. Despair can be produced by circumstances, other people, long-held belief systems, or our own personal tendencies. Sadly, no matter how hopeful we may be by nature, we will all face times when the glass really does appear to be half empty, or even to have fallen to the floor and shattered.

Despair is particularly difficult to endure because it breeds in the sufferer a sense of futility, a feeling that things will never change for the better. Despair looks to the future and sees nothing worth pursuing. It offers the lie that there is no hope. Obviously, despair destroys passion since there is no reason to pursue a better future if one does not exist. Despair can be paralyzing because it presents the belief that nothing we do can change our circumstances, so why even try?

Being married to a husband like Nabal certainly could have led Abigail into a pit of despair. Besides the poor treatment Abigail undoubtedly received from Nabal, she probably also worried about her family and future with a man who was known for his mean spirit and foolishness. It would be only a matter of time until he insulted the wrong person, and, as the story shows, David was that wrong person. Yet Abigail does not act like a woman who has lost hope; instead, she acts quickly and decisively and averts disaster for her family, encourages David in the Lord, and ends up marrying the future king of Israel. How might Abigail have been able to overcome the temptation to fall into despair?

THE SECRET WEAPON: GENEROSITY

I imagine Abigail's ability to practice generosity gives her the edge in battling despair as she maintains a passionate commitment to the Lord and to His people. What do I mean by generosity? I mean, simply, a desire to invest in God's kingdom and in others. A generous person gives—of herself, of her resources, of her passion—to others. And in this act of giving, she strengthens her spiritual passion and overcomes the paralysis, fear, and hopelessness that accompany despair. Generosity invests in both the present and the future. Generosity says, "I will pour into the person or the situation that is before me because I know that God will work in His power to give a bountiful return on my investment." When we are generous, we are making the statement that we believe in the future, and that declaration of hope is the antithesis of despair. Generosity thus contributes to spiritual passion because it gives our desire new outlets beyond our own lives, and it infuses passion into those around us. The premise for the second half of this book is that passion increases when we direct it outside ourselves, and generosity does that in a powerful way.

But what does authentic generosity look like? It can come in many shapes and sizes. Generosity is when a widow watches the preschool children who live next door so their mother can run to the store. It is when a fourth grader befriends the child who is constantly bullied. It is when we give financial aid to missionaries, pray daily for our hurting friend, offer a room to the homeless, send an encouraging note every week to the teenager in our church who is battling cancer, or persevere in acting kindly toward our own teenager who is battling us. Generosity pours into the lives of others and seeks their best. It recognizes the potential in each person and each situation to be used by God for great things.

As Christians, we recognize that our generosity is not founded on our own personal strength, abilities, or resources, but on the reality of God's generosity toward us, as well as His unlimited power. We know that He loves us, that He is active in our lives, and that He has the sovereignty to work all things for our good, and this knowledge gives us the confidence to be generous. We do not have to worry about running out of assets, saving up for a rainy day, or embarking on a project that we cannot finish. Quite simply, we can live in liberality as children of a king with infinite resources instead of as beggars with nothing to draw upon, and this reality makes us generous. We can afford to invest in the lives of others because God has invested everything in us.

Authentic generosity requires this mindset. Ask yourself a question. How do I handle situations in my life or the lives of others that might lead to despair—do I call upon and rejoice in a God who holds the universe in His hands like a child of the king, or do I embrace fear and privation like a homeless orphan with no hope in sight? Abigail shows us how to embrace generosity, even in the midst of a desperate situation, as she invests herself in the life of her husband and family to save them from catastrophe, and in the life of David to save him from unnecessary bloodshed and discouragement.

GENEROSITY IN THE HERE AND NOW

Generosity that increases passion and changes lives operates in both the present and the future. Let's consider generosity in the present first. When it operates in the here and now, generosity meets needs because it focuses solely on the other. Abigail has two people who need her in the present moment—her husband Nabal, whose family and property are about to be obliterated by a fighting force of four hundred men, and David, who in his despair and discouragement is about to commit an act that he will regret for the rest of his life. Abigail will use her generous spirit to invest in the lives of both men, changing each of their present circumstances for the better.

Abigail's first generous choice as she focuses on the one she is helping is to completely disregard her own needs. This is Giving 101, right? It is impossible to give to someone else if we are more concerned about what we need, how we will appear to others, or how we can best protect our resources. According to the biblical story, Abigail "acted quickly" to protect her husband and their family when she heard that David was coming to attack Nabal. I must admit that I might have taken a couple hours to "pray" about whether God wanted me to let my wicked husband face the consequences of his unwise actions! Perhaps this could be Abigail's moment of escape from a life with Nabal. Instead, Abigail immediately seeks to save her husband. She sends two hundred loaves of bread, two skins of wine, five prepared sheep, about sixty pounds of roasted grain, a hundred cakes of raisins, and two hundred cakes of pressed figs to David as he is approaching Nabal's property, and then races to meet him herself. When she reaches David, Abigail falls on her knees before him and asks him to forgive both Nabal, whom she acknowledges to be foolish, and herself, who she admits did not see the men that David had sent. David accepts both her gifts and her apology.

Apologizing for someone else's mistake is one of the most mature ways of disregarding your own needs as you help someone else. Abigail wastes very little time or energy assigning blame or complaining about Nabal to David and his men; she is completely focused on helping Nabal avoid catastrophe. She is also focused on helping David. By meeting David's need for supplies, she bravely accepts the wrath she will certainly face from Nabal for giving away his possessions and disobeying his orders behind his back. Giving to others requires that we disregard our own needs and focus solely on the one in whom we are investing.

I will admit that I really do enjoy using the fancy coffeemaker I gave my husband last Christmas. Because, seriously, he didn't really want those wireless headphones he actually asked for, did he? And spending more time and money than I care to admit on making sure my son's model was the best in the fourth grade was not really for my own reputation in the school, right? He really *wanted* it to have running water and working lights, didn't he? And throwing a slight fit when I did not get the credit I deserved for helping another instructor develop the new curriculum for our university's freshman writing program was not wrong. Surely receiving credit for hard work is only being honest? Does it really hurt to mix in a little something for ourselves when we're giving to others?

Well, these humorous (and, unfortunately, only slightly exaggerated!) examples point to how often our generosity gets mixed up with our own wants and needs. Abigail, however, focuses on the ones she is trying to help, sacrificially suppressing her own desires and fears in the process.

In addition, Abigail works hard to personalize her assistance to both Nabal and David, giving each exactly what they need, even if they don't know it themselves. I'm sure Nabal would not have asked her to go and pacify David, yet that is what saved his life. Maybe Abigail should have listened to the book she had just read on wives submitting to their husbands and let Nabal's own bad choices come back upon his head. But Abigail takes seriously her calling as Nabal's wife and helpmeet, to use the term from the old King James Bible, and so she acts on his behalf in exactly the way he needs. For David, as well, Abigail provides personalized assistance—supplies that are nutritious and will travel in the desert as well as the respect and honor that he so desired but did not receive from Nabal. Generosity that is customized for the person we are investing in reveals forethought and genuine caring.

By personalizing our care for others and by disregarding our own needs, we offer generosity in the present that will meet the needs of those for whom we are caring. And when needs are met, lives are changed, including our own. Abigail's generosity saves her household from catastrophe and stops David from committing a slaughter he would have lived to regret. Abigail's refusal to sink into despair allows her to pour herself passionately and generously into both her family and the heir to the throne of Israel, saving and transforming lives in the process.

GENEROSITY IN THE FUTURE

I had been feeling pretty good about our son's two-year-old checkup at the pediatrician's office until the doctor started reading off a checklist. Can he button his own shirt? Well, no, not exactly. Does he regularly use thirty words or more? Um, he seems to get by with only about six words and a handful of grunts. Has he learned to sit quietly in his high chair at the dinner table? Yes! Well, only if I let him throw food during the meal. Does he help you around the house with simple tasks? Certainly! If tackling the dog is considered a simple task. With a sigh, I realized that my son was already considered behind schedule on the toddler checklist of accomplishments. Guess our hopes and dreams for him would have to be adjusted!

Our culture loves to evaluate and label people as quickly and permanently as we can. A close friend of mine was labeled "delayed" in her mental development at age four, then identified as gifted and talented the next year. My son received the award for "Most Enthusiastic" every single year of elementary school, a euphemism for "most disruptive student in the class" if ever there was one. Our neighbor's son was labeled the franchise player of the high school basketball team until he stopped growing. As a college professor, I've seen students carry labels such as attention deficit hyperactivity disorder into their early twenties. And I've been labeled myself in ways that were often laughably inaccurate and, at other times, hurtful and discouraging.

But labels can actually work in a positive way when they are focused on pointing us toward our potential instead of pointing out our faults. Many of us have experienced having someone believe in the promise in us when the current reality was not so hopeful. A teacher who noticed our capacity for leadership, a coach who recognized our commitment to hard work, a parent who affirmed our caring heart toward others. These are the people who invested in our future on the basis of our potential. It's like the coach who nicknames his player "Champ" before the athlete wins even one competition. The coach is speaking to who he believes the athlete really is, a champion performer, and relating to him in that way, even though reality hasn't caught up yet.

This type of faith in a person's potential is what I like to call generosity in the future. Generosity can meet pressing needs in the present, stoking passion and changing lives. But investing generously in the future can be even more powerful. When we seek to be generous toward someone or a situation in a future sense, we envision the future that is possible and relate accordingly.

Stephen King, one of America's most successful novelists, enjoyed seeing his novel *It* made into a movie that set box office records on its opening weekend.[5] The story of King's early days as a struggling writer, however, is well known and instructive. Barely keeping his family of four off welfare by working as a teacher, writing three hours a night in the family's cramped laundry room, while his wife Tabby cared for the kids and worked at Dunkin' Donuts, King had published several stories in men's magazines, but had little to show monetarily for the effort. When offered a second position at his school that could make ends meet more easily, King was surprised when his wife asked him not to take the additional position so he could continue to have time to write. She believed in him.

Soon after, King began writing a story about a young girl who is teased at school and vows revenge, but threw away the first three pages of the manuscript, deciding he could not write convincingly from a female perspective. Tabby, herself a writer, literally rescued the pages from the trash and persuaded him to try again. With Tabby's help, King finished the novel that would become *Carrie* and launched a career worthy of the Medal of Distinguished Contribution to American Letters in 2003.[6] One person can make a difference in our lives when they label us according to our potential and invest generously in our future. Telling your husband to refuse a second, much-needed source of income because he is a "writer," when his writing consists of a handful of published stories in men's magazines and three hours of effort each night in the laundry room seems a little crazy. But believing generously in the future of others can look crazy simply because it does not fit with current reality. If it was current reality, we wouldn't need belief, right?

God is the perfect example of investing in the future of others—He is intent on meeting our present needs, but He also seeks ways to invest in our future by relating to us in terms of the person He knows we can become. This is why the angel of the Lord addresses Gideon as "mighty warrior" before he has even picked up a sword, why Jesus calls Peter the rock upon which He will build His church before the disciple denies Him three times, and why Mary is honored by Elizabeth as the mother of God before she has even birthed the Messiah.[7] This is also why God persistently sees us as His redeemed, beloved children even when we have been the most wayward.

Our heroine Abigail generously invests in David's present when she honors him personally and provides much-needed supplies for his men. However, her investment in David's present is slight compared to how generously she blesses his future. As we've seen, David is in a bad place. Before his confrontation with Nabal, he had just encountered Saul and his army of three thousand men in the Desert of En Gedi. Finding Saul alone in a cave, David sliced off a piece of Saul's robe while the king was unaware. Choosing not to kill Saul at that moment revealed David's strength and faith in the Lord, but that strength is beginning to fail him now as he hides in the Desert of Maon, mourning the death of the prophet Samuel and struggling to meet the needs of his six hundred men. His greatest supporter is dead, the wife of his youth Michal has been given to another man upon his absence, and he is a fugitive from his homeland, with no end in sight to his wanderings. Nabal's refusal to share his bounty with David, as well as the wealthy man's demeaning insult to David personally, are the last straws for David. He sets his mind to massacre an entire household.

Abigail invests generously in David and his future in several ways. First, she reminds him of his true identity—the anointed King of Israel. She addresses him as "lord," instead of "servant" as Nabal did, and she relates to him as a king by kneeling before him. She announces that David will enjoy a "lasting dynasty" and will be appointed "ruler over Israel."[8] Abigail is not distracted like Nabal was by David's current situation as a penniless, powerless fugitive. She appears to recognize David's true identity in the Lord and relates to him in that way.

What might such a generous investment in another's identity look like in our world today? Well, at the most basic level, we know that everyone we meet is created in the image of God. So perhaps the harried cashier at the grocery store deserves our patience. We know that every person can receive forgiveness from the Lord if they seek it. So maybe we won't make that joke about the pastor in our city who lost his ministry over a personal failing. And we know that a new, successful future is possible for anyone who chooses to repent and follow Jesus. So maybe we will continue to pray for and encourage that ne'er-do-well sibling who seems to turn everything he touches to dust.

Or maybe we will ask God to show us His heart for someone in our lives in a more specific way, enabling us to speak and act toward them in a manner that pours into their identity more concretely. Do you see the gift of evangelism in your close friend? Relate to him as you would an evangelist—encourage his ministry to non-Christians, remind him of how well he shares his life and the gospel, offer to pray with him for those to whom he is seeking to witness. See him as an evangelist, as Abigail saw David as a king. Have you recognized your daughter's sensitive heart toward others? Encourage her to support her friends when they are in need, read a book with her on praying for others, teach her how to release to the Lord the pain she sees in others' lives so she can learn not to carry it herself. When we relate to others according to their general or specific identity in Christ, we are investing in their future and affirming the plans God has to prosper and bless them.[9]

But living up to our identity in God can at times be difficult and draining. Homeless and hungry in the Desert of Maon, David is suffering the very real repercussions of seeking to pursue his identity as God's chosen king of Israel in the face of King Saul's resistance. So Abigail goes beyond simply reminding David of his identity in God. She also reminds him of God's promises toward him. She reminds him that his life will be "bound securely in the bundle of the living by the Lord," while the lives of his enemies God will "hurl away as from the pocket of a sling."[10] Abigail affirms to David that God will bring him "success" and will accomplish "every good thing he promised concerning him."[11] As believers, we all face times when we need someone else to remember the promises God has made to us in Scripture and through the Holy Spirit. We can choose to stand with our brothers and sisters and recall those promises as Abigail did with David, affirming the Lord's goodness and trustworthiness despite threatening outward circumstances or our own internal struggles. Is one of your friends or family members struggling right now with despair because they are losing hope that a promise of God will come to pass? Step in and invest in their future by reminding them of God's faithfulness. Pray with them according to God's promise. Text or call them weekly to remind them of God's goodness. Share your confidence in God's promises with them as they wait for the fulfillment of God's word.

Third, encourage the loved ones in your life to act according to their identity and promises. Abigail gently reminds David that as the future king of Israel, he has been called to "fight the Lord's battles," so no "wrongdoing" should be found in his conduct.[12] Abigail does not berate or shame David for the anger and hurt he is feeling, but she advises him to resist the temptation to take revenge on Nabal by pointing to his future:

> When the Lord has fulfilled for my lord every good thing he promised concerning him and has appointed him ruler over Israel, my lord will not have on his conscience the staggering burden of needless bloodshed or of having avenged himself.[13]

Abigail knows that David's identity as the imminent king of Israel requires him to act in a manner that honors and obeys God so the people will respect him and trust that he will lead them in the way of God's favor. Slaughtering a household because of a single insult will not keep David on God's path and will not encourage confidence among the people he will be leading. David must act according to his true identity and the promises God has given him instead of allowing his injured pride to determine his course of action. David recognizes this truth in the words of Abigail and praises the Lord for Abigail's intervention.

Have you ever had to remind a Christian brother that he was not living in a manner consistent with his calling? Have you ever been forced to confront a sister who was making choices that detracted from the work God had called her to do? Have you ever had to ask forgiveness of a friend or family member when you allowed yourself to speak or act in ways that were inconsistent with your identity as a follower of Christ? Investing generously in the future of others means that at times we must take the challenging step of speaking truth in love when the Spirit has prompted us to intervene. It is not a job to be undertaken lightly, and it is a job that we usually would like to avoid if we could. Abigail gives us a helpful model for how to approach an erring Christian: rather than berating them for their current unfortunate choices, gently remind them of their calling and promises in Christ and suggest a path that is more in line with who they are and what God is doing in their lives. Placing the focus on the blessings that come from acting in harmony with our identity makes obedience appear much more attractive than the alternative.

Abigail's final investment in David's life is supremely moving and powerful: she chooses to personally connect herself with David and his future. After Nabal's death, David sends messengers to Abigail to ask her to be his wife. David is a homeless fugitive, living with six hundred men in the desert, attempting to stay alive as King Saul marshals the country's elite soldiers to find and destroy him. David has nothing but a promise from God and an act of anointing by a now-dead prophet to support his claim to the throne. Yet Abigail is willing to leave her life and home to join David as he pursues the fulfillment of God's promises to him. Now that is a serious investment! Being generous toward others will often require that we, too, invest ourselves in their lives. Praying for the single parent down the street is more powerful when joined with a weekly invitation to dinner. Sharing encouraging Bible verses with the coworker who is navigating a custody battle is fortified by our invitation to assist with a project that is requiring him to work late nights. Giving monthly support to a missionary in our nearby inner city is augmented by a weekend trip to clean and paint her apartment. Seeking to share the good news of Jesus with a casual acquaintance is aided by the development of an authentic, caring friendship. Connecting ourselves personally to another gives immeasurable force to the investment we have made in both their present and their future.

During my time as a graduate student, my advisor was a great example of a man who connected himself with others personally as he worked to further their success. He took every opportunity to help me achieve my goals. He introduced me to influential people in our field, he asked me to participate in panels he chaired at academic conferences, and he even invited me to contribute an essay to a book that was being published in honor of his professional achievements. After I finished my degree and sought to publish my first book, he continued to offer advice on my work and connected me with his personal associates in the publishing companies of our discipline. He was a wonderful professional model for me of a man who was committed to personally investing himself and his reputation into those he desired to succeed.

Of course, the Lord Jesus is the perfect example of someone who is willing to identify with those He is seeking to bless, taking on human likeness and coming to earth personally to save us. He invested himself completely through His life and death, making the way for the Holy Spirit to be deposited in those of us who follow Him today. Thus, we, like the New Testament apostle Paul, can pour ourselves out as a "drink offering" into the lives of those who are despairing and losing sight of God's precious promises.[14] We do not need to fear depletion or deficiency as we act generously toward those whom God loves. It is a joy and privilege to invest ourselves in God's precious, beloved children as we partner with his Holy Spirit in building the kingdom of Jesus.

A RICH RETURN

Investing generously in others with an eye toward both the present and the future can bear tremendous fruit. Perhaps most importantly, despair is defeated in both the giver and receiver when generosity is released. In our story, David's hope in the Lord and in His promises are renewed by Abigail's investment in his life. He is strengthened to believe again in his identity as God's choice to lead Israel. Sometime after his encounter with Abigail, he again meets King Saul and his army, this time in the Desert of Ziph, and once again David spares Saul's life when he sneaks into Saul's camp and finds the king and his soldiers asleep.[15] David has returned to a place of trust in the Lord and faith in his own destiny. Abigail's investment has paid off in the future king's life.

For Abigail, her generosity actually creates a new future. After the Lord strikes down Nabal, Abigail is not only freed from her difficult husband, but she is joined to David, the Lord's anointed who will lead the kingdom of Israel. Talk about stepping into an exciting future! And their union bears even more fruit—a son. Investing in others always brings us a blessing that is greater than what we originally invested. God's returns are always a safe bet! Instead of a life of pain and despair, Abigail's generosity has given her a new reality of hope, promise, and a legacy.

That being said, we are all familiar with stories of those who generously invested in others and did not end up marrying a handsome, God-fearing, Psalm-singing king. We live in a fallen world, so pouring into others will not always result in a windfall for us or even success for them. People make their own choices, and sometimes those choices are unwise, despite our best efforts to help and encourage. But that is okay. We serve a God who will take care of our needs and will watch over the ones we love, so we can leave the results to Him. Our calling is to use the vast resources of love, kindness, and faith that He has given us as His children to generously invest in those around us, hoping they will embrace the opportunities for growth and blessing that the Lord lays before them.

Whenever I contemplate the idea of truly selfless giving, a scene in Hannah Hurnard's well-known allegory *Hind's Feet on High Places* usually comes to mind. As poor, timid Much-Afraid is learning to trust the Chief Shepherd and discovering how to live in his Kingdom of Love, she watches a majestic waterfall as it pours itself over a cliff and drops to the earth to be "dashed in pieces on the rocks below." Much-Afraid is struck by the joyful abandon with which the droplets of water fall from dizzying heights to the earth, and she listens in wonder as the droplets sing:

From the heights we leap and go
To the valleys down below,
Always answering to the call,
To the lowest place of all.

As the Chief Shepherd explains, the water droplets are made to leap over the cliff and fall in an "abandonment of self-giving," joining together in small rivulets at the bottom and continuing their flow, always downward, downward to the lowest place.[16] We, too, as followers of the Chief Shepherd, find our highest joy and purpose in investing ourselves generously in others, releasing God's power in their lives and sharing the blessings of His love and mercy. It is our destiny to pour into others as God has poured into us.

But perhaps the most exciting aspect of Abigail's story for us as modern believers is that powerful results are produced by only a rather modest investment. Abigail did not single-handedly end preindustrial hunger, bring world peace, or even place David on the throne. She simply invested in a small way in the person and situation in front of her, and mighty consequences followed. As someone once said, "In this life we cannot always do great things. But we can do small things with great love."[17] How often do we hesitate to take a step of generosity because it seems like it is too small and insignificant to make a difference? It is a misconception in our society that only great works of extensive influence change lives. As Christians, we know that God can bring stunningly abundant blessings from our simplest acts of obedience. Saved from a seemingly small act of revenge that in reality could have derailed his God-ordained destiny, David goes on to found a dynasty in Israel that ultimately produces the Savior of the world. When we partner with the Lord of the universe in building His kingdom through investing in others, He opens the floodgates and pours out more than we expect or even hope for. Even the slightest act of kindness will make a difference in our lives and in the world. Starting small is a great way to begin living a more generous life; it will produce immediate fruit and will lead to the development of a giving spirit.

Who can you touch today? Can you think of a situation in which you could set aside your own needs and minister to someone else? Can you think of someone who could use a personalized act of generosity this week? Has God placed on your heart a person who has forgotten her true identity in Christ? Do you have a friend who needs to be reminded of God's promises, or encouraged to live a life more in line with his potential as a child of God? Is God calling you to connect personally with someone to help him step into the future God has planned for him? Opportunities to invest generously are all around us. Let's follow the Holy Spirit and invest in God's work of expanding His kingdom throughout the world through generosity. Our passion for God will not only grow, but will multiply as a result.

CONCLUSION

MAKING CHANGES

The godly characters featured in this book have shown us how passion flows out of a life of godly discipline. We have seen a marginalized widow ward off discontentment through unceasing devotion to God, a mother demonstrate unswerving courage as she saves her sons from a life of slavery, a princess maintain then falter in her faith in the face of assailing doubt, and a prophetess step into her destiny to lead her people into the breathtaking future God has for them. And we've seen a city saved from destruction through initiative, the stifling status quo of a crowd resisted through a refusal to conform, barriers destroyed by tenacity, and generosity overcome crippling despair.

Did one or more of these characteristics resonate with you? Are you eager to take steps toward a more passionate pursuit of God? Any excitement for change and growth that the words of this book have sparked in you can now become stepping-stones in your path toward greater spiritual passion for our loving Lord. We need only take the first step to begin.

As you consider how God might want you to start applying the ideas you have encountered here, let me give you one piece of encouragement: *God's plan for each believer is a life of sustained, powerful, transformative growth.* As Paul prays for the Christians in Colossae:

> We continually ask God to fill you with the knowledge of his will through all the wisdom and understanding that the Spirit gives, so that you may live a life worthy of the Lord and please him in every way: bearing fruit in every good work, growing in the knowledge of God, being strengthened with all power according to his glorious might so that you may have great endurance and patience, and giving joyful thanks to the Father.[1]

The presence of the Holy Spirit in our hearts ensures that we will mature—that is His job! Jesus Himself said the Holy Spirit would lead us into truth, convict us of sin, and comfort and encourage us. So, if some of the ideas in this book have sparked a desire in you to grow in your passion for the Lord, know that growth is not only possible, but it is God's Plan A for His children. We can expect it and rejoice in it!

Here are a few brief suggestions that I have used to apply new truths to my own life. Perhaps you will find some of them helpful. First, make a plan for growth that is both focused and concrete. Focus your plan by choosing one attribute that you responded to and asking the Holy Spirit to begin to work in your heart regarding that attribute. Don't try to work on every characteristic at once and don't expect to reach full maturity in even one quality right away. Next, make your plan concrete by determining one or two practical steps that you can take to begin to develop that characteristic in yourself. Perhaps start with one or two of the steps suggested in this book. A plan that is focused on a specific goal and that incorporates concrete steps is much more manageable than one that tries to accomplish everything at once, and it gives us a practical path forward that is not overwhelming.

Second, take action according to your plan. I know this seems obvious, but often this is where we fail. Ask the Holy Spirit to give you the self-discipline to act on your focused, concrete action plan. As we know from the New Testament writer James, "As the body without the spirit is dead, so faith without deeds is dead."[2] You don't need to be particularly wise or gifted or even spiritually mature to carry out your plan. And you don't need to do it perfectly the first time or even the fiftieth time. Just keep doing it!

My last suggestion for implementation is perhaps the most important point in this book, and I'm not exaggerating. If you remember anything from these pages, please recall that everything we do as children of God takes place within the centrality of our relationship with Him. God loves us. He is on our side. *He* is passionate about *us*. Supremely passionate. Passionate enough to endure the pain and shame of the cross to bring us to Himself. His ultimate goal for us is to help us grow in intimacy with Him.

What this means for us is that any steps we decide to take to grow in our relationship with God should never feel oppressive or threatening. We should never view our attempts to mature as a burden or as something that God will hold against us if we fail. His love really is unlike ours in that it is perfect and not based in any way on our performance. If we ever begin to feel that we are unworthy of God's love, that we have wasted too much time and too many opportunities, that we have messed up too badly for forgiveness, or that we have delayed too long to make a fresh start, we must remember that these ideas are not from God, but are from Satan. Here is the truth about every believer in Christ:

> And we all, who with unveiled faces contemplate the Lord's glory, are being transformed into his image with ever-increasing glory, which comes from the Lord, who is the Spirit.[3]

With God's perfect love for us as our foundation, we can pursue growth and change with joy and confidence. The Holy Spirit lives in us to guide and help us, Jesus is interceding for us in heaven, and the Father surrounds us with His love and presence in the midst of our struggles and successes. See yourself as a redeemed child who enjoys the boundless affection and resources of a loving God, and you will know in your heart of hearts that growth is your destiny and birthright.

If receiving and believing in God's love for you is a significant struggle in your life, I would suggest that you begin applying the truths of this book with the attribute of devotion in the first chapter. Growing in devotion will give you a firm cornerstone on which to build when you pursue maturity in the other characteristics. Once we have a strong, personal foundation in God's love, we will find less confusion, uncertainty, and backtracking when we seek maturity in other areas because our intimacy with God bears the fruit of understanding, clarity, and confidence. Certainly we will struggle our whole lives with getting better at connecting with God and receiving His love, but if you suspect you need to do some foundational work in this area before you move on to the other characteristics, begin by focusing on devotion.

Perhaps the most exciting truth about personal spiritual growth is that our maturity impacts not only us as individuals but also the church of Jesus Christ and the world. As we each play our roles and become more passionate lovers of God, we will pursue blessing and loving others with greater enthusiasm and more powerful results. Our partnership with the Holy Spirit to build the kingdom of Jesus in a world that desperately needs Him gladdens the heart of God immeasurably and extends His purposes far beyond our own individual lives.

Thank you for taking the time to read this book and join with me in reflecting on how we can deepen our spiritual passion. Allow me to leave you with a reminder of who we are in Christ and the life we are called to lead:

> [Jesus' death for sin] means that anyone who belongs to Christ has become a new person. The old life is gone; a new life has begun! And all of this is a gift from God, who brought us back to himself through Christ. And God has given us this task of reconciling people to him. For God was in Christ, reconciling the world to himself, no longer counting people's sins against them. And he gave us this wonderful message of reconciliation. So we are Christ's ambassadors; God is making his appeal through us.[4]

How beautiful and significant is the life of the follower of Jesus! Embraced by God and used by Him to reach a lost world for Christ—this is our privilege and joy. As we grow in the godly characteristics that generate spiritual passion, we will see our excitement for God and His purposes grow and deepen along with our intimacy with Him. I hope this book has helped you in your journey to passionately pursue the God who is more than worthy of our adoration, our obedience, and our lives.

DISCUSSION

01

DISCUSSION

- Name three words you would use to describe someone who is devoted to something. Would you use those words to describe your relationship with God?

- Can you describe a time when you struggled with discontentment? What was the most difficult part of that struggle?

- What moves you the most in a corporate worship service? What elements of worship have been a blessing to you in your own personal worship times?

- Have you ever fasted? Describe what you learned from the experience.

- What is a limitation in your life currently that you would like to move beyond? How might increasing your devotion to God give you the passion to move past that limitation?

APPLICATION

- Listen to or sing along with one or two worship songs at the beginning of your devotional time.

- Write a letter to God sharing something that is on your heart.

- Skip one meal and instead read Psalm 145, meditating on God's goodness.

GOING DEEPER

- Read the autobiography of St. Thérèse of Lisieux, a twenty-four-year-old French Carmelite nun who focused her short life on being devoted to God.

- Commit to fasting one day every week for one or two months. Notice how God uses this discipline to reveal the things that control you.

- Memorize several Psalms of praise; use them to meditate on God's loveliness and beauty as a regular part of your devotional time.

02

DISCUSSION

- In what areas of your life do you experience the most fear—finances, health, relationships, work?

- Describe a time you saw the ripple effect of fear in your life. What others areas of your life were affected?

- Share about a time you moved forward with courage despite fear. Were the results what you had expected?

- Describe a personal experience with God that has been a source of encouragement to you. Have you shared that experience with others?

- What helps you strengthen your trust in the Lord? What role does your church or other fellowship group play in bolstering your faith?

APPLICATION

- Memorize one or two verses from Scripture that encourage us to have courage in the face of fear—try Deuteronomy 3:16, Isaiah 43:1-2, or John 16:33.

- Pray with a friend about something you believe God is calling you to do. Ask the Holy Spirit to reveal to you one simple step you can take to move forward with courage in that area and have your friend pray for success as God leads you.

- Identify one person you know who has shown courage in a fearful time—a health challenge, family crisis, professional setback. Ask that person to lunch to share with you what they learned through their fearful experience.

GOING DEEPER

- Memorize Psalm 91. As you recite this Psalm, meditate on the words of promise and comfort from God.

- Read a biography of a courageous person—Abraham Lincoln, Jan Hus, Joni Eareckson Tada, Lin Zexu, Amy Carmichael. Learn from their brave choices.

- Volunteer to serve for six months in a ministry at your church that is outside your comfort zone. Notice the ways in which you are challenged and grow.

03

DISCUSSION

- How has your spiritual life been affected by doubt? Can you identify a specific experience with doubt and its effects on you?

- How do you hear God best? What role do these practices play in how you hear God—Bible study, meditation, Scripture-based teaching, input from friends?

- Which is more difficult for you—acting decisively by faith or waiting patiently for God's timing?

- Do you struggle with believing that God loves you and always acts in your best interests? Brainstorm ways you can develop a more accurate picture of God's consistent desire to love and bless you.

- How would you describe the connection between faith and freedom? Recall a time you experienced the freedom that comes from trusting God.

APPLICATION

- Read Psalm 73. Share with the Lord any details of your life that are causing you stress. Tell Him you trust Him to work out those details in His own way and time, then spend a few minutes enjoying His presence as Asaph did.

- Make a list of twenty ways God has blessed you over the past six months. Be specific and think creatively. Celebrate these blessings in a new way, perhaps by dancing, singing, drawing a picture, or shouting praise.

- Identify one promise you believe God has given you and write that promise on an index card. Place the card in a visible location and every time you see it, declare out loud to God your assurance that He will accomplish that promise.

GOING DEEPER

- Consider these words of Julian of Norwich, a late-fourteenth-century English Christian and the author of the earliest surviving book in English by a woman: "Some of us believe that God is almighty and may do everything, and that he is all-wisdom and can do everything; but that he is all-love and wishes to do everything—there we stop short. It is this ignorance, it seems to me, that hinders most of God's lovers."[21] In partnership with the Holy Spirit, plan a few simple steps to help you grow in trusting God's perfect love for you. Ask God to forgive you for the times you have not trusted Him.

- Practice silence in your interactions with others for two days. Speak only when you have to and focus your comments on things of importance. Notice how silence helps us learn to release the details of our lives to God.

- Ask your spouse, best friend, child, or another important person in your life to share with you one promise they believe they have received from God that has not yet come to pass. Commit to praying in faith for that promise regularly, both by yourself and with that person.

04

DISCUSSION
- Describe a personal vision you have had professionally, relationally, spiritually, or in another area of your life. How did it come to fulfillment?

- Can you deduce any elements of God's current call on your life? Are there parts of yourself that need to be brought in line with that calling—your thoughts, words, or behavior?

- Think back to a time you experienced significant growth in an area of your life. What helped you grow the most during that time? What was the biggest challenge?

- What do you think holds most people back from stepping into something new? What holds you back?

- Can you identify the part of God's vision process that is most applicable for you right now—call, preparation, fulfillment? Pray for the courage and wisdom to move forward in that area.

APPLICATION
- Ask the Holy Spirit to help you pinpoint some areas of your call. Use some of these methods to identify elements of your call: make a list of what you are good at, ask a friend to identify your strengths, recall areas in which you have experienced success, try a new ministry at your church.

- Read or listen to one teaching on a topic that you are seeking to grow in. Take notes on that teaching and identify two practical changes you can make to grow in that area. Commit to working on those two changes for the next month.

- Evaluate one area of your life that has stayed constant for the past several years. Ask the Holy Spirit if it is time to make a change.

GOING DEEPER

- Evaluate where you currently spend your time, money, energy, and other resources. Are any of those areas outside your current call? Make a plan to reorient your life and resources around your current call from God.

- Identify a person who evidences maturity in an area that relates to your call. Make a connection with that person through a mentorship, shared ministry involvement, scheduled prayer time, or some other experience through which you can learn. Dedicate six months to learning and growing with that individual.

- The Bible uses many pictures to present God's truth. Ask the Holy Spirit for a picture that represents God's vision for you. Recall that picture every morning and acknowledge the truth of God's vision. Watch for experiences that reveal how God is bringing the reality of that picture into your life.

05

DISCUSSION

- Do you tend to be an initiator or a reactor? Why do you think you have this tendency?

- What are some of the hardest things about being first?

- Describe a time you struggled to get God's perspective on a situation in your life. Can you recall specific promises of God that helped you develop His mindset?

- Do you agree that concrete actions are necessary to accomplish spiritual goals? Why or why not? Recall a time you achieved a spiritual goal by taking concrete steps.

- What obstacles tend to hold you back from finishing what you have initiated—lack of self-discipline, misdirected focus, fatigue, loss of hope? Brainstorm ways to overcome those obstacles.

APPLICATION

- Identify one area of your spiritual life in which you desire to grow. Develop and implement two concrete steps you can take to grow in that area. Evaluate your progress after six weeks.

- Make a list of the times you have been willing to risk in order to move forward into new opportunities. Spend some time thanking the Lord for His faithfulness during those situations.

- Add one new element to your personal devotional time, such as singing praise songs, reading a devotional classic, praying for others, taking a walk, or taking communion. Evaluate how initiating that new element affects your time with the Lord.

GOING DEEPER

- Pray about beginning a new ministry in your church. If you feel led by the Lord, ask your church leadership if you can begin the ministry on a trial basis.

- Initiate a new relationship in your life, perhaps mentoring a younger Christian, serving a non-Christian neighbor, or supporting a leader in your church through prayer. After six months, evaluate how the Lord has used this new relationship in both of your lives.

- Using your Bible and perhaps a biography, study the life of the New Testament apostle Paul. Evaluate the ways Paul initiated ministries in the Gentile world.

06

DISCUSSION

- What strikes you the most about what the woman in Luke 7 did? Why?

- Share a time when you resisted conforming to those around you. Did you accomplish your goals?

- Have you ever been out of step with other Christians? What was the most difficult aspect of that situation?

- Can you describe a time you made a significant sacrifice for God? What were the results?

- What helps you break with long-standing traditions in your life and adopt new perspectives?

APPLICATION

- Read a Christian book that is written by someone outside your Christian tradition—evangelical, Catholic, mainline, charismatic, etc. Identify the new ideas that you encounter.

- Compile a list of what makes you unique—spiritual gifts, personality traits, life experiences, passions and desires, and more. Thank God for making you who you are in Christ.

- Ask the Holy Spirit to reveal to you ways in which you have judged other believers. Repent of those judgments and spend some time praying for the Christians whom God places on your heart.

GOING DEEPER

- Identify one way you conform to others in an unhealthy way at church, work, home, or your neighborhood. Ask the Holy Spirit to show you one thing to do to change that, and follow His suggestion for three weeks. Evaluate the results.

- Consider something that you could sacrifice to the Lord—time to devote to ministry, hurt feelings from a painful encounter with someone, demands for respect from your supervisor, money you have saved for a personal purchase. Pray about sacrificing what the Lord brings to mind.

- Make a list of ways you can respond to God physically—fasting, serving others, adopting a new style of worship. Try one new physical response to God each week for the next month.

07

DISCUSSION

- How tenacious are you? Do you tend to give up easily or do you battle until you are successful?

- Describe some normal responses people have to intimidating barriers. What is your typical response?

- Can you describe a time you experienced God's silence and how you reacted to it?

- What helps you persevere in faith when you face challenging, scary times?

- Have you ever pressed past an answer of "no" from God? What were the results?

APPLICATION

- Memorize Hebrews 12:1–3 and recite those verses every time you face a situation that requires you to persevere. After two weeks, evaluate if you have become more aware of the need to persevere in difficult situations.

- Create a list of your top three usual responses to difficult situations. Brainstorm ideas on how to adjust each typical response to make you more tenacious.

- Identify one area of your life in which you are not hearing clearly from God. Spend ten minutes each day with the Lord for one week, listening for the Spirit's direction in that area.

GOING DEEPER

- Spend some quiet time with God, asking the Holy Spirit to bring to your mind any wrong beliefs you have about God's commitment to you. Do you doubt His love for you, His pride in who He has made you to be, or His dedication to your growth and healing? Ask God's forgiveness for your wrong thinking and ask the Holy Spirit to bring to your mind scriptures that correct your beliefs and encourage you. Perhaps memorize those scriptural passages.

- Recall a dream you have relinquished. Seek the Lord to determine if you gave up too soon. Listen to hear if the Holy Spirit reignites the dream and redirects your approach.

- Make a commitment to act immediately on any guidance you are given from God for one month. Follow through on that direction, even if you are unsure about it. Evaluate how your ability to hear God and your faith grow during this time.

08

DISCUSSION

- Describe a recent situation in which you struggled with despair. What related emotions did you experience during this time?

- What do you think acknowledging and embracing God's generosity toward us looks like in a practical sense? Is this your usual response to God's goodness?

- Which is easier for you when giving to others—disregarding your own needs or personalizing your giving?

- Describe a time someone invested in your future. What was the most significant part of that investment for you?

- What do you consider some major obstacles to Christians embracing their true identity in Christ? How can we overcome them?

APPLICATION

- Commit one act of generosity every week for the next month. Increase the frequency to two times per week in the following month.

- Write a thank-you note to someone who has invested in your life. Be specific in sharing with them how their investment changed you and your future.

- Make a long-term commitment to generosity: financially support a child in need, join a service ministry in your church, begin a friendship with someone new.

GOING DEEPER

- Prayerfully create a timeline of God's important acts of generosity in your life. Examine each incident in which He invested in you and thank Him for the fruit.

- Meditate on your true identity in Christ. Discern specific characteristics of who God has made you to be and ask the Holy Spirit to show you if you have been living and thinking in a manner consistent with those attributes.

- In partnership with the Holy Spirit, decide on one act of sacrificial giving that you could perform. After executing the act, spend time evaluating the emotions produced in you by your action and the ways in which you can grow in giving.

ENDNOTES

INTRODUCTION

1   John Maxwell Team, Twitter post, December 9, 2016, 12:54 p.m., https://twitter.com/JohnMaxwellTeam.
2   Harry S. Stout, *The Divine Dramatist: George Whitefield and the Rise of Modern Evangelicalism* (Grand Rapids, MI: Eerdmans, 1991), 281.
3   George Whitefield, *George Whitefield's Journals* (Carlisle, PA: Banner of Truth Trust, 1960), 476.

CHAPTER 01

1   Song of Songs 4:9a; 7:10.
2   Song of Songs 8:6a.
3   Alistair Magowan, "Borg on Federer," *BBC Sport*, June 24, 2007, http://news.bbc.co.uk/sport2/hi/tennis/6758285.stm.
4   Prov. 4:23.
5   Luke 2:36–38.
6   For a more detailed description of the temple courts, see "Second Temple: Court of the Women," *Bible History Online*, accessed August 7, 2017, http://www.bible-history.com/links.php?cat=52&sub=4912&cat_name=Second+Temple&subcat_name=Court+of+the+Women.
7   James 4:1,2a.
8   Nick Vujicic, *Life Without Limbs: Inspiration for a* Ridiculously *Good Life* (New York: Doubleday, 2010), viii.
9   Vujicic, *Life Without Limbs*, x.
10 New King James Version.
11 Song of Songs 4:12; 4:16.
12 James 3:11.
13 New International Version 1984.
14 Anne Graham Lotz, *My Heart's Cry: Longing for More of Jesus* (Nashville, TN: Thomas Nelson / W Publishing Group, 2002), 56.
15 1 Pet. 2:9.
16 Twila Paris, *In This Sanctuary: An Invitation to Worship the Savior*, with Robert Webber (Nashville, TN: Star Song Publishing, 1993), 67.
17 While I have been unable to find the exact location in Augustine's writings where these words originally appear, I have read this quotation in many secondary sources. See, for example, Richard J. Foster, *Prayer: Finding the Heart's True Home* (San Francisco, CA: HarperSan Francisco, 1992), 1.
18 Foster, *Prayer*, 13.
19 Rom. 8:16.
20 Richard J. Foster, *Celebration of Discipline: The Path to Spiritual Growth* (New York: HarperCollins, 1978), 42.
21 I have not located this quotation in Forster's writings, but it is common in other sources; see, for example, Eugene H. Peterson, *Subversive Spirituality* (Grand Rapids, MI: Eerdmans, 1997), 38.
22 Joyce Huggett, *Open to God: Deepening Your Devotional Life* (Downers Grove, IL: InterVarsity Press, 1989), 14.
23 Foster, *Celebration*, 49. Foster's chapter on fasting is a good place to start to understand and begin practicing this Christian exercise.
24 *The Norton Anthology of American Literature*, ed. Nina Baym, vol. A, *Beginnings to 1820*, ed. Wayne Franklin, 8th ed. (New York: W. W. Norton, 2012), 597. The philosopher cited is Alfred North Whitehead.
25 John Woolman, *The Journal of John Woolman*, in *The American Tradition in Literature*, eds. George Perkins and Barbara Perkins, vol. 1, 12th ed. (Boston: McGraw-Hill, 2009), 211.
26 Isa. 27:3.

CHAPTER 02

1   Virginia Woolf, *To the Lighthouse* (San Diego: Harcourt/Harvest Books, [1927]), 59-60.
2   Kevin E. Vowles, Lance M. McCracken, and Christopher Eccleston, "Patient Functioning and Catastrophizing in Chronic Pain: The Mediating Effects of Acceptance," in "Mediation and Moderation," special issue, *Health Psychology* 27, no. 2 (2008): S136, http://web.ebscohost.com.lib.pepperdine.edu/ehost/pdfviewer/pdfviewer?sid=a4a6647c-3607-4316-83e6-e5005 5accb15%40sessionmgr4004&vid=2&hid=4104.
3   1 John 4:18.
4   Franklin Delano Roosevelt, Inaugural Address (address, United State Capitol, Washington, DC, March 4, 1933), http://historymatters.gmu.edu/d/5057/.
5   *A History of Western Society*, vol. C, *From the Revolutionary Era to the Present*. eds. John P. McKay and others, 10ᵗʰ ed. (Boston: Bedford/St. Martin's, 2011), 876-881.
6   Ambrose Redmoon, "No Peaceful Warriors!" *Gnosis* 21 (1991): n.p., quoted in Julia Keller, "The mysterious Ambrose Redmoon's healing words," *Chicago Tribune*, March 29, 2002, http://articles.chicagotribune.com/2002-03-29/features/0203290018_1_ chicago-police-officer-terry-hillard-courage.
7   2 Kings 4:2-4.
8   2 Kings 4:7b.
9   Matt. 25:14-30.
10   Carlos Coto, "True Believer," *Nikita*, season 3, episode 3, directed by Danny Cannon, aired November 2, 2012 (Burbank, CA: Warner Bros. Television).
11   2 Cor. 9:8.
12   Eph. 3:20.
13   Isa. 61:3. Jesus' reference to this passage from Isaiah can be found in Luke 4:16-21.
14   Job 42:5-6 (New Living Translation).
15   Ps. 78: 4, 7.

CHAPTER 03

1   2 Cor. 4: 8-9, 13-14.
2   Ol Parker, *The Best Exotic Marigold Hotel*, directed by John Madden (London: Blueprint Pictures, 2012), DVD.
3   2 Cor. 4:16a, 18.
4   "Since we live by the Spirit, let us keep in step with the Spirit." (Gal. 5:25)
5   John 10:27 (King James Version).
6   See 1 Sam. 19:9-17 for the story.
7   James 2:24, 26.
8   Ps. 73:16, 17.
9   Ps. 73:23, 24.
10   See 2 Sam. 3:12-16 for David and Michal's reunion and 2 Sam. 5:1-5 for David's anointing as king of Israel.
11   See 2 Sam. 6:12-19 and 1 Chron. 15:25-28, 16:1-6 for the story of the ark's return to Jerusalem.
12   2 Sam. 6:20b.
13   2 Sam. 6:21b-22a.
14   Ezek. 37:1-3.
15   Ps. 52:8b.
16   Ps. 56:9b (New Living Translation).
17   Ps. 54:6-7.
18   See 2 Sam. 7:20, specifically; the entire prayer is found in 2 Sam. 7:18-29.
19   2 Sam. 6:23.
20   2 Cor. 1:20.
21   Julian of Norwich, *Revelations of Divine Love*, ed. Halcyon Backhouse with Rhona Pipe (London: Hodder and Stoughton, 1987), 150.

CHAPTER 04

1   Hadley Malcolm, "M&M's promises new flavors, textures as brand turns 75," *USA Today*, March 3, 2016, https://www.usatoday.com/story/money/2016/03/03/mms-75th-anniversary/81173224/.
2   David A. Kaplan, "Mars Incorporated: A pretty sweet place to work," *Fortune*, January 17, 2013, http://management.fortune.cnn.com/2013/01/17/best-companies-mars/.
3   Ibid.
4   See 1 Pet. 1:20 and Eph. 1:4 for both uses of "before the creation of the world."
5   Gen. 3:15.
6   James Hudson Taylor, *China's Spiritual Need and Claims* (London: Morgan and Scott, [1865] 1884), 1, https://archive.org/details/pts_chinasspiritualn_3720-1090.
7   Prov. 29:18 (King James Version).
8   This story is told in Exod. 1:15–2:10.
9   Tyndale House Publishers, *Chronological Life Application Study Bible* (Carol Stream, IL: Tyndale House, 2012), 1531 n Acts 9:23, 1557 n Gal. 1:15–24.
10   Exod. 4:29–31.
11   Sara Groves, *Conversations*, INO Records, 2000, compact disc.
12   Num. 12:1–15.

CHAPTER 05

1   Matt. 13:1–23.
2   Prov. 3:27, 28 (New International Version 1984).
1   2 Sam. 20:14–22. This chapter focuses on a woman who in a desperate wartime situation advocates for a violent, deadly solution. I am not in any way advocating violence or devaluing the trauma of lethal situations, but simply focusing on her act of initiative during a time of hostile conflict.
2   Nic Young, *The Bible*, directed by Crispin Reece (Century City, CA: 20th Century Fox, 2013), DVD.
3   Job 42:2.
4   2 Sam. 20:18–19.
5   2 Sam. 20:16.
6   1 Cor. 12:12–27.
7   Thomas Paine, *Common Sense*, in *The Norton Anthology of American Literature*, ed. Nina Baym, vol. A, *Beginnings to 1820*, ed. Wayne Franklin, 8th ed. (New York: W. W. Norton, 2012), 641, 642.
8   Zech. 4:10a.
9   "William Wilberforce," Christian History, August 8, 2008, http://www.christianitytoday.com/ch/131christians/activists/wilberforce.html.

CHAPTER 06

1   *In Search of History: Salem Witch Trials*, CD-ROM. Lionsgate, 1998.
2   Frances Hill, *The Salem Witch Trials Reader* (Cambridge, MA: Perseus Books Group, DaCapo Press, 2000), 81.
3   Ibid., 85.
4   Ibid., 80.
5   Ibid., 80.
6   Prov. 29:25.
7   See verses 11–19.
8   Luke 24:10–11.
9   Acts 10:34, 35. See Acts 10 and 11 for the complete account.
10   Rom. 14:19.
11   See Luke 7:36–50 for the complete episode.
12   Luke 7:37.
13   Luke 7:47b.
14   See John 12:1–8 for the story of Mary of Bethany's action.
15   John 21:22.
16   C. W. Andrews, ed., *Memoir of Mrs. Ann R. Page*, Women in American Protestant Religion, 1800–1930 (New York: Garland Publishing, [1856] 1987), 26. Spelling and grammar have been silently modernized in all quotations from Page's writings.

17   Ibid., 31.
18   Ibid., 65.
19   1 Cor. 4:16–17, 20.
20   C.S. Lewis wrote that we often are erroneously persuaded "that the bodily position makes no difference to [our] prayers; for [we] constantly forget … that whatever [our] bodies do affects [our] souls." C. S. Lewis, *The Screwtape Letters*, rev. ed. (New York: Macmillan Publishing Company, Collier Books, 1982), 20.
21   Col. 1:24.
22   2 Cor. 2:15.
23   Luke 7:50b.

CHAPTER 07
1   Kelli Anderson, "Duel Meet," *Sports Illustrated*, July 23, 2012, 66.
2   Amelia Lee Duckworth, "The Key to Success? Grit," Internet video, TED Talks Education, April 2013, http://www.ted.com/talks/angela_lee_duckworth_the_key_to_success_grit.
3   See Matt. 15:1–20 and Mark 7:1–23.
4   Matt. 15:14a.
5   Matt. 15:16–18.
6   The complete episode is told in both Matt. 15:21–28 and Mark 7:24–30. The woman's words are quoted from Matt. 15:22b.
7   Matt. 15:23.
8   Matt. 15:23.
9   Matthew Henry, *A Commentary on the Whole Bible* (Iowa Falls, IA: World Bible Publishers, n.d.), 5:219.
10   Matt. 15:24.
11   See, for example, Henry, *Commentary*, 5:218, and William Hendriksen, *New Testament Commentary, Exposition of the Gospel According to Matthew* (Grand Rapids, MI: Baker, 1973), 622.
12   Matt. 15:26.
13   Matt. 15:27.
14   Matt. 15:28.
15   William Hendriksen, *New Testament Commentary, Exposition of the Gospel According to Mark* (Grand Rapids, MI: Baker, 1975), 293.
16   For Abraham, see Gen. 18:16–33; for Moses, see Num. 14:1–25; for Mary, see John 2:1–11.

CHAPTER 08
1   1 Sam. 25:10, 11.
2   1 Sam. 25:31.
3   2 Sam. 3:3a.
4   1 Sam. 25: 3; 25:1; 25:25.
5   Seth Kelley, "Box Office: Stephen King's 'It' Officially Opens to Massive $123 Million," *Variety*, September 10, 2017, http://variety.com/2017/film/news/it-box-office-stephen-king-movie-opening-weekend-1202553361/.
6   See Stephen King, National Book Foundation's Medal for Distinguished Contribution to American Letters Award 2003 Acceptance Speech (speech, New York, November 19, 2003), http://www.nationalbook.org/nbaacceptspeech_sking.html#.Uz2aAPldXSh, for King's perspective on his wife's influence on his life.
7   Judg. 6:12b, Matt. 16:18, Luke 1:42–44.
8   1 Sam. 25:25; 1 Sam. 25:28; 1 Sam. 25:30.
9   Jer. 29:11.
10   1 Sam. 25:29.
11   1 Sam. 25:30, 31b.
12   1 Sam. 25 :28b.
13   1 Sam. 25:30–31a.
14   Phil. 2:17.
15   1 Sam. 26 :1–25.
16   Hannah Hurnard, *Hind's Feet on High Places* (Wheaton, IL: Tyndale House / Living Books, 1987), 184–185.
17   Although often attributed to Mother Teresa of Calcutta, these may not be her authentic words. See, for example, Mother Teresa of Calcutta Center, "What You Should Know," *Motherteresa.org*, last modified July 19, 2010, http://www.motherteresa.org/08_info/Quotesf.html#2.

CONCLUSION
1   Col. 1:9b-12a.
2   James 2:26.
3   2 Cor. 3:18.
4   2 Cor. 5:17–20a (New Living Translation)

5 OTHER TITLES FROM SQUARE HALO BOOKS

The Beginning: A Second Look at the First Sin
"[A] very readable and engaging discussion on the nature and consequences of the original sin using the biblical accounts as his primary authority … A sound background in scripture, a solid presentation of his positions, and generous application make this book a very good reference on the subject." —*The American Journal of Biblical Theology*

Deeper Magic: The Theology Behind the Writings of C.S. Lewis
"… a treasure trove of systematized information—a must for every C.S. Lewis fan, and all the rest of us who should be."—Norman Geisler, PhD

Intruding Upon the Timeless: Meditations on Art, Faith, and Mystery
"A collection of brief essays by the editor of *Image*, a distinguished journal of religion and the arts. A nice mix of the whimsical, provocative, and devout, as befits the variegated subject."—*First Things*

A Book for Hearts & Minds: What You Should Read and Why
"Curators of the imagination, stewards of the tradition, priests of print, [Hearts & Minds Bookstore has] always done more than sold books: they have furnished faithful minds and hearts. This book is a lovely testimony to that good work."—James K.A. Smith, Calvin College, author of *You Are What You Love: The Spiritual Power of Habit*

Good Posture: Engaging Current Culture with Ancient Faith
"The Row House Forum serves the public good in one of the best ways possible: by promoting ideas, art, conversation, and human flourishing. It's a gift to the local community, as well as a gift from the local community to the world."—Karen Swallow Prior, author of *On Reading Well: Finding the Good Life Through Great Books*

SQUAREHALOBOOKS.COM